Jack Fassett

A Memoir of Essays

For Margaret —
My neighbor and friend with
kind regards —
Jack Fassett
10/5/14

Jack Fassett

A Memoir of Essays

———— ∞ ————

John D. Fassett

Graphics by Joy Mermin

CHAPEL HILL
PRESS, INC.

ISBN 978-1-59715-108-5
Library of Congress Catalog Number 2014948228

First Printing

Dedicated to Betty, Joy, Jack, and Lora

CONTENTS

Betty and Jack, 1977

INTRODUCTION

This obviously is not a typical memoir. It is not a chronological recitation of the events of my life. Rather it is a recounting of a number of separate factors that have each had a significant impact on my life. I previously wrote a more typical form of memoir covering the early years of my life, titled *The Shaping Years: A Memoir of My Youth and Education*, published by Xlibris in 2000. I also wrote a volume titled *Betty: Chronicle of a Moving Life*, published by Chapel Hill Press in 2008, about my beloved wife, which inevitably incorporated much data regarding my activities during the more than sixty years covered by the book during which we were inseparable. Betty died on November 16, 2013. I began writing this different form of memoir shortly after.

Six months earlier Betty had been admitted to Duke Hospital with extreme shortness of breath. The doctors at Duke discovered that she had a large, inoperable mass in her left lung—probably cancer. As she strongly desired, rather than being sent to Croasdaile Village Retirement Home's nursing facility, Betty was allowed to return to our apartment in the Village. It had been our home for fourteen years. Betty was allowed to return there on the condition that she be under hospice care, and that she have around-the-clock attention either from our daughter Joy, from me, or from home-care medical assistants.

Despite the facts that she was constantly on oxygen and either in her hospital bed or her special wheelchair, Betty continued smiling, was mostly convivial with her medical caregivers, and maintained a positive attitude until the end. She particularly liked being transported in her wheelchair by one of her caregivers to an exercise class, a neighborhood or Parkinson's group meeting, or just to the entry of our building where she could greet all arrivals with a few words and a smile. She played serious games of Scrabble on her computer with Joy regularly up until a couple of weeks before her death. She was very coherent two nights before she died. She also obviously was aware that the end was near. As usual, I fed Betty her nine o'clock medications as soon as the night caregiver, who took over until seven in the morning, arrived. As I kissed Betty on her forehead and said goodnight, she asked me, "Is everything set at Arlington?" I assured her that the arrangement that we had agreed to some years before for both of us to be inurned together in the Columbarium at Arlington National Cemetery would be carried out.

On the Saturday night that she died, we were alone. Her daytime caregiver had departed at six o'clock and her nighttime caregiver did not arrive until nine. Just before her daytime caregiver left, I had given her the syringe of morphine provided by hospice to ease her labored breathing. As I kissed her forehead, she whispered her last words to me: "You know, I love you." I held her hand. At 7:25 p.m., she quietly gasped a couple of times and just ceased breathing.

The major reason I began writing these essays was to keep busy after Betty was gone. The hospice bereavement counselor strongly advised that immersion in writing had proven to be a very effective way to cope with grief. I am writing this introduction just two weeks after Betty's service at Arlington on June 18, 2014. Essay 11 recounts my trip to Arlington with Betty's ashes and her flag and the impressive service conducted prior to the insertion of Betty's ashes into our niche in Court 9 of the Columbarium.

Appropriately, Essay 11 is the final one in this memoir.

Jack Fassett
July 1, 2014

Jack Fassett

A Memoir of Essays

Oliver (Levi) Fassett

Mary Fassett

David Darby

Lena Darby

CHAPTER 1

Roots

It appears to be settled that my original American ancestor was Patrick Fassett. My son located Patrick's tombstone in an old graveyard in Billerica, Massachusetts, and made a rubbing of it for me when he was doing gravestone rubbings while attending Brown University. The framed rubbing still adorns my hallway wall. It reads, "Here Lyes Ye Body of Patrick Fasset aged 85 Years Who Deceased November The 6, 1713." Jack's search was inspired by a volume written by Katherine Fassett Shuster and published in 1974 titled *The Fassett Genealogy: Descendants of Patrick and Sarah Fassett*. Mrs. Shuster included an entry titled "Canadian Born Fassetts," which identified my ancestors with the comment, "It is not surprising to find Fassetts born in Canada just over the border from Vermont and New Hampshire."

While Mrs. Shuster's sources agreed that Patrick Fassett "was a Scot named Patrick Macpherson," they diverge on the story of his arrival in America. One stated that he "came to New England about 1652, one of a group of prisoners taken in Cromwell's campaign against the Scots." Another stated that Patrick "was descended from a family named Macpherson, refugees from Scotland, who fled to Ireland to escape religious persecution. To conceal their identity, they assumed the name Faset, sometimes spelled Fawcett or Fossett. Patrick came to this country with his wife Sarah, from Rock Fassett Castle in Ireland and settled in Lexington, Mass." When Betty and I toured Ireland in 1990, we searched diligently for Castle Fassett, including consulting a historian at

Trinity College in Dublin, but were unsuccessful in locating the castle. The historian advised us that so-called castles were prolific and that over time Castle Fassett probably became just a pile of rocks.

One fact is clear. Patrick and Sarah had a large family, which certainly accounts for the wide dissemination of their surname. An apparently reliable source stated that Patrick, "a prudent and well behaved farmer acquired considerable estate conveying land to his sons in his lifetime." Mrs. Shuster's tome lists ten offspring of Patrick and Sarah, seven sons and three daughters, commencing with John born in 1670 and concluding with Benjamin born in 1690. One son, Samuel, died young, and their next child was also named Samuel. The six surviving sons all had wives and a lot of children. None of their sons apparently is directly responsible for the Canadian Fassetts, but many in succeeding generations of Fassetts moved north as well as west from Massachusetts to establish new roots.

My mother's contribution to Mrs. Shuster's book identified Oliver Fassett (sometimes written as Olivier Fassette) as the beginning of our line. She states that he "lived in and around Montreal," "he was a police chief," he married Julia Asher, and they moved to Warren County in upstate New York where Oliver became an American citizen in 1877. Oliver and Julia had four children, two boys and two girls, all born in Glens Falls. Their firstborn was my grandfather, Oliver David Fassett, born in 1871. Oliver, often known as Levi, spent his entire lifetime in Glens Falls.

Glens Falls was the most northern community of any size in eastern New York. It was located along the upper Hudson River, and it contained a large paper mill with its product made from logs floated to the mill on the river. It also boasted a factory that manufactured men's shirts and one of the first life insurance companies in America. Glens Falls' greatest fame, however, derived from being the setting of some of the most important events in James Fenimore Cooper's novels, including *The Last of the Mohicans*. Located below the bridge spanning the river between Glens Falls and South Glens Falls was a rocky islet that contained the hiding place known as Cooper's Cave. Glens

Falls also produced an eminent lawyer, Charles Evans Hughes, who served as governor of the state, was a candidate for president in 1916, and ultimately became one of the nation's great chief justices of the Supreme Court.

My grandfather was employed in the shirt factory for a period, and he subsequently worked in construction, where he became a skilled carpenter. As a young man he married Lillian Ball, and they had two daughters, Lillian and Ida, born in 1893 and 1895, respectively. His wife died in 1895, and the two girls were raised by their maternal grandparents. Levi subsequently married Mary Lamoureau, a member of a large, devoutly Catholic, and French-speaking Glens Falls family. Mary's sister, Lena, who had never married, had become the owner of the Lamoureau home, a two-family house at 13 Montcalm Street, only a few blocks from the Catholic Church. She welcomed Levi to the home. Lena had long been employed in the shirt factory in town. After she retired, Lena walked to service at the church every morning. Much of the conversation between Lena and Mary and with their neighbors was in French.

Levi and Mary spent their entire lives in the Montcalm Street home, living on the first floor with Lena occupying the large second-floor bedroom as long as she lived. The young couple had their first child, Mabel, in 1897; their second child, Howard John, in 1899; and their second daughter, Evelyn, in 1901. All three of the Fassett children were raised in the Catholic tradition, and Howard and Evelyn attended the Catholic school in Glens Falls. At a very young age, Mary had what was probably a stroke; thereafter she was always confined to her bed or to a rocking chair where she regularly recited her rosary while fingering her beads. Mabel, though still quite young, had to assume the major responsibility for her mother during the day while her dad worked, and Howard and Evelyn attended school. Levi became employed as the weigh master at a large quarry located along the Hudson River between Fort Edward and Glens Falls where large quantities of limestone were mined.

Howard and Evelyn proved to be good students in the Catholic school system. He became valedictorian of his graduating class in 1916. His valedictory address dealt with the nation's recent problems with Mexico. Probably with help from his Aunt Lena as well as a scholarship, Howard began college in the fall of 1916 at Colgate University in Hamilton, New York, as a member of the class of 1920. Evelyn also went on to the State Normal School in Plattsburg, to train to be a teacher after she graduated from high school. Mabel cared for her mother, Mary, until she died in 1940 and thereafter also cared for Levi until he died in 1947. My strongest recollections about attending the funeral of my grandmother as a youngster are that my grandfather insisted on taking me to a clothing store in town to purchase a suit with long pants for me, so that I would be properly attired during the ceremony. I also remember sitting in the Catholic church for a long service in a language I was unable to comprehend. My grandfather's funeral occurred after I was discharged from the air corps and back in college, and I was not able to attend. When I next visited Glens Falls, I visited his grave and was surprised to see that his stone identified him as Oliver Fassette.

In her early years of caring for her mother, Mabel met a devout Catholic lad from Fort Edward named Charles Culligan. After service in the trenches of France during the Great War, he returned to Glens Falls to continue his courtship of her. As a veteran, he was employed by the state as the leader of the three-man crew overseeing the maintenance of the Champlain Canal, a waterway with a pair of locks connecting the Hudson River and Lake Champlain. It was an important water route between Canada and New York, and Charlie and his crew traversed it regularly in their small craft, taking depth readings to anticipate silting problems. Because of Mabel's devotion to taking care of her mother and then her father, though he visited her virtually every evening of the year and always joined the Fassetts for Sunday dinner, Charlie and Mabel did not marry until 1948 after both Mary and Levi had expired. It must have been close to the all-time record for length of a courtship.

After a year at Colgate, Howard, along with many of his classmates, volunteered to serve in the fledgling Naval air corps. He spent his short military career at the newly developed Floyd Bennett Field on the south shore of Long Island. After his discharge at the end of the war, he lived with one of his father's sisters in Bristol, Connecticut, and was employed on a factory production line until he could resume his education. He then graduated with the class of 1921 from Colgate. When he graduated, he accepted a position in the Lindenhurst, Long Island, school system as a high school teacher and basketball coach. When he moved to one of the two boardinghouses in Lindenhurst that catered to teachers, he met several of his future colleagues, including a blonde, blue-eyed recent graduate of the State Normal School at New Paltz named Irene Darby. She had been hired to be a third-grade teacher in the elementary school. Howard liked his dinner mates at the boarding-house, but he detested the food the owner served. He particularly disliked sauerkraut, which was included as a major item at each dinner meal. Having heard reports of a better menu at the other boardinghouse, he moved there as soon as he conveniently could.

Fanny Irene Darby disliked her given first name and never used it. She had been born and raised in the town of East Hampton, a lovely oceanfront com-munity about twenty-five miles from Montauk Point, the easternmost point on Long Island. Before going to New Paltz, she had graduated as one of a handful of girls who constituted the 1919 graduation class of East Hampton High School. The only boys who had been in the class had left to serve in the war. Her only sibling, an older brother named Arthur, had not attended the high school. He had become intrigued at an early age by that emerging form of transportation, the automobile. He went west to Cincinnati, where many of his mother's rela-tives resided, to seek a job. He wanted to be either a chauffeur or to work in one of the machine shops where his other male relatives were employed.

Arthur's mother's relatives consisted of various branches of the Boehme family that had gradually all emigrated from Leipzig, Germany, seeking new opportunities during the last quarter of the nineteenth century. Several of the males were fine craftsmen with wood, and others were experienced in the developing toolmaking business. Arthur and Irene's mother, Lena Boehme, emigrated as a young woman and found employment as a nursemaid for one of the more affluent Cincinnati families. In the latter part of the nineteenth century, many affluent families chose as their favored summertime residence the pleasant conditions on or near several lakes of upstate New York, particularly Lake George. During a summer sojourn at Lake George, Lena Boehme met a young liveryman named David Darby.

David Darby was the youngest son of a large English family from the area of Britain around Birmingham that was fast becoming industrialized. He was only remotely related to Abraham Darby, the builder of the first iron bridge, which became the symbol of the beginning of the Industrial Revolution. David's father died early, and his mother had remarried. The opportunities for a young man with little education were very limited. Neither the ministry nor India were possibilities for him, so his mother arranged for him to immigrate to the United States and find employment with an older relative who had immigrated and was operating a livery stable in a coastal town of New Jersey. There David rapidly became adept at handling and training horses and at driving various kinds of wagons and carriages. He was at Lake George providing hired service to affluent residents of the summer resort when he and Lena Boehme met.

After a relatively short courtship, David and Lena, a very ambitious young couple, decided to wed and to start their own combination livery and boardinghouse business. They recognized that the days that Lake George would be the prime summer location for wealthy American families were dwindling. With their employers they had both had occasions to make visits to the fast-emerging acme of summer vacation spots near the ocean along the south shore of Long Island. Lena had become aware that many of the affluent families of Cincinnati, including the Procters and Gambles, were building summer homes in the area known as the Hamptons. The Long Island Rail Road had been extended from New York City to Montauk, making relatively rapid transportation to the Hamptons quite feasible.

The Darbys purchased a multiacre tract of wooded land fronting on Appaquogue Road, which was less than half a mile from one of the choicest stretches of white-sand beach on the southern side of Long Island. Appaquogue Road ran off the main carriage highway bisecting the south fork of Long Island from Riverhead, through Southhampton, Wainscott, and Sagaponack. It made a left turn at the East Hampton Town Pond and proceeded through Amagansett to Montauk Point. Montauk Point contained the impressive lighthouse with lights warning and welcoming ships heading for New York harbor, the harbor of the fishing village on the north side of Montauk Point, or those heading down Long Island Sound toward the once-active whaling village of Sag Harbor.

Once David and Lena took ownership of their new property, they oversaw the building of a very substantial wooden structure, consisting of many horse stalls at the ground level and living quarters for the Darbys, the stable employees, and other boarders at the second. Arthur had been born in 1900, and Irene became a member of family in 1901. By then, the Darby livery stables were a bustling enterprise with many horses in the stables, a variety of carts and carriages for rental, and a number of employees and temporary guests. To feed everyone, Lena was constantly busy in her kitchen, making bread and pies and preparing meals. Not long after Irene arrived, the Darbys decided to separate their abode from the stables and the help, and one of the original buildings was moved to the front of the lot and expanded to create a two-story, five-bedroom home with large living, dining, and entry rooms plus a large kitchen with an adjacent pantry. The home contained a dirt-floored cellar that could be entered either from a trap door in the kitchen close to the large black stove and oven. or from another trap door at the rear of the house. In addition to a well, two large cisterns were dug to store rainwater from the roof and drains, and to supply water to the home. The cellar contained many shelves, which were filled with large quantities of fruits that Lena preserved in season. Applesauce from the several apple trees on the property was always in good supply, and beach plum jelly from the plums picked from trees growing wildly in the dunes were Lena's specialties. The cellar was also the location of a couple of large pottery crocks filled with hens' eggs collected from the chicken coop and stored in a viscous substance to be available for baking when the hens were not laying.

One of David Darby's sidelines while operating the stables was teaching young people to ride. He took groups of his students on supervised rides along the beach and nearby. The students were children of summer residents. Irene did not get to accompany any of those groups, and she was not an accomplished horseback rider. However, when she got old enough, she had her own pony and cart, and she had many experiences driving that rig. She also was given a parrot, which she taught to say a few words. During her youth, a colony of artists built homes farther down Appaquogue Road near Georgica Pond, a saltwater pond behind the dunes. It was periodically replenished when storms sent ocean water over the dunes. Irene enjoyed being invited each year to a Christmas party at the home of artist Thomas Moran, and throughout her life she cherished a rendering she received from him of the falls of the Yellowstone River.

Irene attended East Hampton's school and graduated from high school in 1919 with a small all-girl class. She corresponded with one of her classmates during her entire life. She took piano lessons as a child and enjoyed playing her whole life. She treasured a large collection of sheet music featuring mostly popular tunes of World War I ("Over There," "Lili Marlene," "Yaphank Blues," "I Didn't Raise My Boy to Be a Soldier"). One of her favorite memories was of when the campaign of presidential candidate Charles Evans Hughes visited East Hampton, and she was selected to play the piano during the proceedings.

After high school, Irene attended New Paltz State Normal School in the town of New Paltz on the west side of the Hudson River between Newburgh and Kingston in lower New York State. She made many friends there and became a loyal member of the Arethusa Sorority. During the two-year course she trained to be an elementary school teacher. They taught the Palmer method of cursive writing. She had beautiful handwriting all of her life. Upon graduation from New Paltz, Irene accepted a position as a third-grade teacher in the school system in Lindenhurst, Long Island, a town on the south side of the island in Suffolk County, just east of the Nassau County line and about sixty-five miles west of East Hampton. The roads in Suffolk County were not yet generally well-paved in 1921, so a trip from Lindenhurst to East Hampton then was a challenging three-hour journey. Irene's parents presented her with a new Ford automobile as a graduation present so that she could make the trip home to see them. She recounted many tales of getting stuck on muddy roads or of the headlights on the car falling off or failing on those trips.

In accordance with custom, upon arriving in Lindenhurst for her first teaching job, Irene became a boarder at one of the pair of boardinghouses that catered to teachers. Initially, one of her fellow boarders was Colgate graduate Howard Fassett, who also was a novice teacher, but at the high school. He also had been employed to be the coach of the boys' high school basketball team. While Howard deserted Irene's rooming house shortly after the start of the school year because he did not like the food, the friendship between the two novice teachers blossomed. When basketball season began, Irene attended all of the games. She and Howard would read to each other on other nights. She kept a diary of these events, and I recall reading it and being amazed at the extremely low scores in the games.

Despite the facts that Howard had been raised in a strict Catholic family and Irene was not a Catholic (the Darbys had been affiliated with a couple of East Hampton churches and were much more active in the Masons and the Eastern Star), Irene accepted Howard's proposal of marriage before the end of their first teaching year, and they were married by a priest in Lindenhurst. While they had discussed a honeymoon in Europe, the newlyweds had insufficient funds for such a trip. Indeed, after the school year ended, they took a trip to Glens Falls to visit the Fassetts and to Niagara Falls. They were accompanied on their journey by Irene's parents.

Since the Lindenhurst school district prohibited the employment of married women, Irene and Howard found positions during their first year of marriage on the staff of a private educational institution, Kew Forest School, in Queens, a borough of New York City. Their proximity to the city enabled them to socialize with a few of their college and normal school friends who worked in the area, and to sample some of the amenities of the metropolis. Irene's parents much desired them to settle in East Hampton, but a summer there convinced Howard that neither the atmosphere nor the opportunities were attractive. He found work at the Maidstone Club demeaning, and the Darbys' proposal for them to operate a sandwich, pie, and snack stop on the Montauk Highway would have been only a seasonal enterprise, even if attractive. In order to promote this proposal, Irene's father had constructed from old stables a small diner that was named the Dew Drop Inn. Her mother proposed that she would provide the pies and such to be offered at the stop to travelers on the highway. The Darbys assured the newlyweds that the inn would prosper with the increasing presence of automobiles traveling such a main road. That August in East Hampton the Fassetts' first child, Constance Jane, was born.

After only a year at Kew Forest School, Irene and Howard moved to Vineland, New Jersey, where Howard had a plan to combine teaching with operating a chicken farm that produced eggs. They bought three acres of land for their project. Howard had no real experience with farming, but he had read a couple of books about such operations. The chicken farm idea was a flop since Howard was not cut out to be a farmer. The following year Howard began his involvement in the real estate sales business when he commenced doing some farm sales work in the Vineland area for a farm agency with offices in New York and Philadelphia. That led to Sol Beilin, the operator of the business, inviting Howard to join his agency, American Farm Agency, at its headquarters in New York City. To be closer to that new position, the Fassetts moved to Orange, New Jersey. Irene again went to East Hampton for the birth of the Fassetts' second child, John David, on January 30, 1926.

Those are my roots.

Not long after my birth, the Fassetts decided to move to Long Island again to take advantage of the easy commuting to New York City on the Long Island Rail Road and to be closer to East Hampton. They purchased a new home with an FHA mortgage in the development being constructed by the Mott Brothers Builders in Mineola. They selected a three-bedroom house with a sun porch and an oversize lot at 430 Marcellus Road. Their new home was barely a mile from the train station and about ninety miles from East Hampton. It was a bustling community of mostly young people with children.

Much of the foregoing history has been based on my memory. I am sure I have made some mistakes. However, I hope someday a much more detailed history will be written based on the book titled *Some Memories* that Irene wrote for her granddaughter Joy in 1972, a collection of other notes and documents now collected in a big red file, and the great resources for ancestry exploration available these days via the Internet.

War Interruption #1—World War II

War Interruption #2—The Korean War

CHAPTER 2

My Nemesis—Educational Interruption

During my youth one of the popular radio and newspaper items was Robert Ripley's "Believe It or Not," which often reported the surprising number of happenings of some event. It occurs to me that, if my experience with scholastic interruptions had been reported to Ripley, I might have qualified for his list of persons who had commenced different phases of schooling in one group and finished with an entirely different group.

Most of the interruptions of my academic career resulted from personal situations, but the initial one was the result of a wider problem. When I was ready to start kindergarten at my new home on Long Island in 1930, the stock market crash had occurred, and the Depression had commenced with its many ramifications. One of those early repercussions was the decision by our school district to discontinue kindergarten for economic reasons. Accordingly, youngsters of my age, unlike their predecessors, missed that early scholastic experience and were required to wait to begin schooling in the first grade a year later.

I enjoyed two grades with my original classmates in Mineola before our association was abruptly severed shortly after the start of third grade. I had developed a debilitating malady which was diagnosed (fortunately, apparently erroneously) as poliomyelitis. Infantile paralysis diagnoses were at their peak in this country (the disease had received much publicity due to President Roosevelt's affliction and the founding of the March-of-Dimes campaign to fight it). The doctor prescribed that I be kept in bed (my mother had to carry

13

me to medical visits), so I missed that entire year of classes. However, I did not miss learning since my teacher regularly sent to me all of the materials necessary to keep up with the work of my classmates. My mother was a former grade-school teacher, so she supplemented those materials with lessons she provided. Since I had to remain in bed, I had plenty of time to absorb all of the materials with the result that, when the doctors decided I could return to school at the end of the year, I was tested and found sufficiently advanced in all subjects that I was allowed to skip the next grade (a decision perhaps also encouraged by school budget considerations). A major result of this skipped grade was that, from that date until I completed my first year of college, I was always the youngest student in each of my classes.

I spent three pleasant, but very challenging, years—the longest uninterrupted academic stretch in my life—with my Mineola classmates before I moved on again. As I detailed in *The Shaping Years*, those years were challenging because it was the depth of the Depression, my father was either unemployed or on WPA, and I was engaged in various occupations (a magazine route, selling greeting cards by door-to-door solicitation). However, I did engage in some ball games in a nearby field, and I did attempt to learn how to dance at a free dancing class where my mother enrolled my sister and me. I even had my first "date" when I invited one of my classmates (Edna) to the party at the conclusion of the dance classes.

The Depression necessitated my next academic interruption when the mortgage on our Mineola home with its nice lot was foreclosed and we had to move to a much smaller house with virtually no lot in the adjoining town of Williston Park. Our new town had its own elementary schools but bused older children to the Mineola High School. Accordingly, my older sister as a result of the move converted from walking to school to taking crowded bus rides each morning and afternoon. Since our move occurred in late fall 1937, I was assigned to a class scheduled to graduate from eighth grade in January 1939 (Park Avenue School had graduation exercises in January and June each year). While my tenure at Park Avenue was short, it was very pleasant due to a very supportive teacher and very successful since I became valedictorian of my class, much to the consternation of some of my classmates' mothers. However, since all eighth-graders in New York took the statewide regents exams and my ranking was based on those results, there was not much factual basis for their complaints.

After graduation I began catching the school bus with my sister and neighboring kids for the commute to Mineola High School. That routine continued for only two terms (I was busy taking a full schedule of freshman and sophomore courses plus fulfilling a job as a painter on late afternoons and Saturdays). In the summer of 1940 my grandmother, who had been ill and tended much of the time by my mother, died, and my mother consented to move to the large Darby homestead in East Hampton (ninety miles out Long Island from Williston Park) with all three of us children (my older sister and I had been joined by a much younger sister in November 1935).

Since I had spent many happy summer vacations and other visits to East Hampton throughout my youth, the transition to becoming a year-round resident was not difficult, and transferring from a huge high school (more than one thousand students) to one in a small town (only a few over two hundred students) was actually quite pleasant. Since there were no midyear classes, it was decided based on my academic record that I would enter East Hampton High School as a junior, even though I had completed only half of my sophomore year in Mineola.

One of the highlights of my entry into the new school was being asked to join the football squad and actually playing first-string right guard for the second half of the team's six-game season. Most of our opponents were much larger towns (Southampton, Riverhead, Greenport) plus a private military academy and we were fortunate to win two games, but I relished the evolving friendships including with the new, young coach, a recent graduate of my father's alma mater, Colgate University.

My father never joined us living with my grandfather in East Hampton. After a year of incapacity as a result of a serious operation while we resided in

Williston Park, he had begun employment with the Metropolitan Insurance Company, and his job location was in mid-island. Accordingly, he lived in a rented room all week and joined us only on weekends. As I began my senior year, my father's work resulted in his moving to Rochester in upstate New York. In order to reunite our family, he rented a nice house in a suburb, and my mother again packed for another move.

I was able to play sixty minutes in East Hampton's September 27, 1941, opening game with Greenport, which we lost, 18-0. My coach talked to my mother about the possibility of me living with him and his young wife in their apartment to complete my senior year, but the proposal did not fly. As a result, a month into the term my mother and I met with the principal of John Marshall High School, located only a few blocks from our new residence, to arrange my transfer there. I had begun classes in advanced algebra, physics, and French in addition to English and American history in East Hampton, but the principal deemed it unrealistic for me to attempt the first three at midterm in a new school. I was permitted to continue my English and history courses, but to replace the others I was assigned to a typing course (where I was the only male) and a retailing course, also in the commercial department. Needless to say, I did not have to work very hard to prepare for my new curriculum, but I did find the English and History courses very satisfying (each was taught by a much older teacher than I had previously experienced). The English teacher shortly began encouraging me to write, and she submitted a poem I produced for a 1942 compilation of writings by high school students. The history teacher promptly realized how closely I was monitoring world events, and commencing shortly after December 7, 1941, he assigned me the task of providing the class each morning with a five-minute report on major world developments. I enjoyed this reporting since I always began my day with the radio absorbing the latest news.

I developed few friendships and had no social life during my year at John Marshall, so I greatly looked forward to beginning college and making some new friends. I had saved enough from my various enterprises (and had $250 Grandma Darby had given me for my "college fund" before she died) to handle the first year's tuition at the University of Rochester if I continued to live at home and commute by bus, and my parents agreed to that plan. True to his offer to my mother as part of the proposal to stay in East Hampton, and despite the rejection of that proposal, Coach Jones did contact Colgate University. I received a communication from them inviting me for an interview to discuss a possible scholarship, but I agreed with my parents that, in view of world and family conditions, attending the U of R made more sense.

As with my prior scholastic endeavors, I managed to complete only the first college year at the U of R before I finally became old enough to volunteer for military service. It was a great year in many ways. I decided to try out for the freshman football squad and succeeded not only in making the first team, but in being selected to practice with the varsity at the end of the frosh season. I developed a number of close friendships and was tapped to become a member of a fraternity that contained many of the school's athletes as well as many scholars. I did passably well in my courses despite the disruptions to college life resulting from the many calls of students to military service, and, despite the impediment of having to commute to the campus during much of the year (during the final few months I was able to occupy a room in the fraternity house that was evacuated by a brother called to active duty by the air corps), I enjoyed a pleasant social life dating a cheerleader and a number of other coeds.

During the spring in 1943, a test was given on the campus jointly by the army and the navy to determine eligibility for their recently announced specialized training programs (A12 and V12). One of the first questions on the test required choosing a preferred branch of service. I checked army (having decided on a political science major) whereas several of my friends checked navy. As a result, those friends, upon enlisting in the navy, were assigned to a new V12 unit at the U of R, which took over and was housed in my fraternity house until the end of the war.

When I first attempted to sign up for the army program, I failed the physical for enlistment due to the mashed nose I had received on the football field, but promptly after classes ended, the medical director for the athletic department arranged for me to be admitted to the medical school hospital and my nose to be operated on so I could breathe normally. It took several weeks for the swelling in my nose to decline and my two black eyes to disappear, so it was August 4 before I passed the physical and was sworn in as a private in the army, thus ending my one-year association with the U of R class of 1946.

Since the fall term was approaching and the Army Specialized Training Program (ASTP) contemplated using facilities of academic institutions, my orders from the army arrived promptly, and they directed me to report to the newly formed unit at Cornell University in Ithaca, New York. When I arrived there I found that I was assigned to a company of men who had all completed at least a year of college (virtually all of the others from institutions in the New York City area, predominately City College). All of the others had undergone some cursory basic training, so I not only had to catch up on military drills and rules, but had to acquire documents, uniforms, and supplies. I also learned that my company was scheduled to pursue a course in "basic engineering."

My company together with a couple of others studying other subjects (one was all graduates studying Oriental languages) were housed in an ancient wooden dorm called Cascadilla Hall. Only our company, consisting of about fifty privates, was required to stand reveille and roll call every weekday morning in the paved area fronting the building. We also were required to stand taps each weekday evening, and we marched the campus somewhat in formation. We strongly resented the latter requirement and envied the other army and navy units assigned to the campus whose troops strolled between classes with the coeds. The army units chowed together in a cafeteria converted to a mess hall in the basement of the student union building. The food was quite good, and my group really enjoyed the availability of virtually unlimited fresh milk produced on the agricultural facilities of the aggie school.

Like all of my other educational experiences, my Cornell days were interrupted. In February 1944, the first month of our second term, like at the U of R, I caused the interruption. Having been a poli-sci major, I was not pleased with the engineering curriculum, so, like at the U of R, the interruption resulted from my own action. I wished for more active military duty. At the time, the army Air Corps was still seeking candidates to be cadets and train to be pilots, navigators, or bombardiers. A small group of A12ers was allowed to take the qualification test when it was given in Ithaca, and as a result, three of us received orders early in 1944 transferring us to the air corps classification center in Biloxi, Mississippi. Thus, I did not complete my second term at Cornell, but unfortunately neither did any of the other members of my company; a few weeks after I departed, the army discontinued the A12 program and transferred all of its personnel to units preparing for Operation Overlord, the Normandy invasion. I later heard that several of my Cornell friends did not survive that operation.

Even my expected air corps educational program was rudely interrupted after only a few months. At Biloxi I took all of the physical, educational, and psychological tests devised to determine qualifications of candidates to become aviation cadets, and I learned that I had received top scores for pilot or navigator training and barely missed a similar score for bombardier training. Those of us who were so qualified were deemed cadets, but we were sent to the air base at Stuttgart, Arkansas, to await further orders. In our new base we were given some instructions in aircraft maintenance, but mostly we performed a variety of jobs patiently awaiting orders. I ended up driving a large airplane fuel truck with another cadet riding its rear while we refueled AT-10 training planes (the base was an advanced twin-engine training base). The one bright spot of my sweltering summer in Arkansas was that, for the first time in my life, I finally got to fly—serving as a crewman on a B-25 while it flew missions testing firebombs by dropping them against a target erected in the middle of a rice paddy adjacent to the Mississippi River.

My relatively brief life as a cadet concluded when an announcement was made to our group that the air corps had decided that it had a surplus of potential trainees, and accordingly, all who had transferred from a different branch would be returned to that branch. Since the ASTP no longer existed, the three of us who came from there were given the options of transferring to the infantry or to one of the other air corps schools. The fellow who had ridden the rear of my truck chose to transfer to radio operators' school; the other one and I chose aircraft gunnery school. In short order he and I were on our way to Lowry Field in Denver, Colorado, to become armorers as a prelude to attending gunnery school in Las Vegas, Nevada. By a quirk of fate, my buddy ended up training on the new B-29 and going to the Pacific theater. I earned my wings and my sergeant stripes training on a Flying Fortress (B-17), but, just as I expected to fly to the European theater, another quirk of fate diverted me to Arizona to teach instrument flying to officers sent to this country to form the foundation for a proposed air force for Chiang Kai-shek's army. As related in my memoir *The Shaping Years*, I spent the balance of my air corps career until my discharge at the end of February 1946 in some interesting and challenging assignments.

With credits for military courses, I was able to complete my U of R tenure and be awarded my degree in just two more years, thus graduating as a member of the class of 1948. I even played another year of varsity football in 1946 and, as a political science major, was astounded at graduation to receive the annual prize for the best work in the English Department. Between the effects of almost three years in the army and the fact that my Betty and I had married in August 1947, after a courtship commencing the weekend after the end of the 1946 football season, I was a far more serious student during my return to the university.

My educational hex revived when Betty and I agreed, after I spent a year as an employee of Aetna Insurance Company, that we could handle the cost and lifestyle limitations of my attending three years of law school. Accordingly, in early September 1949, with our month-old daughter along, we departed upstate New York for New Haven, Connecticut, where Yale had admitted me along with a scholarship and a choice living assignment in a large old mansion near the law school, which had been divided into ten apartments for married students with children.

My first year at Yale went very well, and I was employed during the summer of 1950 by one of my professors to assist him in writing a new textbook. At the end of my World War II service I had been offered and accepted a lieutenant's commission in the army reserve. In June the hostilities erupted in Korea, and the army immediately began mobilizing its reserve units and calling up unattached reservists like me to fill out those units. As a result, my contribution to the book *Contract in Context* when it was ultimately published was minuscule at best since I was included on one of the first orders to mobilize reservists in Connecticut. All of my entreaties about being in school, being a parent, and having served in World War II brought only the response that I was lucky to get in early because a major mobilization was inevitable.

While the unit with which I was mobilized ended up in Korea within a few months, I had the good fortune of being assigned to a position of legal officer and to the staff of the commander of the training battalion at Fort Eustis. During my year at the base near Newport News, Virginia, I prosecuted or defended hundreds of special courts-martial, taught military justice courses, and wrote a number of reports requested by command. Life in Virginia was almost pleasant since Betty and our daughter were able to join me, and our son was born at the base hospital. When I firmly rejected the commander's suggestion that I transfer from the reserves to the regular army, he was understanding and initiated the paperwork that allowed me to return to inactive duty after a little over a year. Reserve commissions had a five-year duration, and I declined to accept an extension of mine even with a promotion.

Having missed one year I graduated with the Yale Law School class of 1953 instead of 1952. The bright side of that final educational interruption was that my class standing did not suffer, and I received the award for top marks. Moreover, at the recommendation of the dean, I was chosen by Associate Justice Stanley Reed to be his law clerk for the 1953 term of the U.S. Supreme Court. It was a life-defining experience not only because of my resulting close relationship with the justice, but because it was the term that welcomed new chief justice Earl Warren and produced the landmark decision in *Brown v. Board of Education*, in which I was able to play a significant role.

ALL EXPENSES ALSO INCLUDED
UNDER WEEKLY EXPENDITURES

DATE	ITEM	FROM	AMOUNT	TOTAL
4-16-46	5 SHIRTS : 3 WHITES	NEW PROCESS Co	10.50	10.50
4-20-46	BLUE STRIPED SUIT	GRAVINS	35.-	45.50
4-20-46	TIE - BLUE CREPE	GRAVINS	1.-	46.50
4-20-46	SHOES - BROWN WINGTIP	EASTWOOD'S	8.95	55.45
4-21-46	TIE - BLUE ARROW	MOM-EASTER	—	—
5-6-46	ENGLISH RIDING BOOTS	SPORTSHOP	11.95	67.40
5-6-46	RIDING BREECHES	SPORTSHOP	4.95	72.35
5-25-46	COVERT TOPCOAT	NATIONAL	42.50	114.85
6-3-46	BLACK FORMAL SHOES	EASTWOOD'S	8.95	123.80
6-4-46	BLACK SOCKS - INTERWOVEN	HALL-COVEL	.65	124.45
7-23-46	WATCH CLIP STRAP	PERLMANS	1.-	125.45
7-23-46	BOOKS-"CANDIDE" "SUN ALSO RISES"	BOOK SHOP	1.90	127.35
9-20-46	SPORTS COAT BLUE	BONDS	20.-	147.35
9-20-46	SLACKS - BLUE	BONDS	8.50	155.85
9-28-46	SUIT GREY TWEED-	BONDS	33.75	189.60
10-10-46	SHIRT - WHITE	BONDS	3.50	193.10
10-10-46	TIE MAROON KNIT	BONDS	1.50	194.60

38   39

A page from my first post-World War II Account Book

CHAPTER 3

Numbers

Unlike most of my classmates in elementary school in Mineola on Long Island in the 1930s, my two favorite subjects were geography and arithmetic. I enjoyed playing with numbers—doing addition, subtraction, division, and multiplication. Both of those interests were enhanced during my bedridden third-grade year when I was taught at home by my mother, who was a former teacher and enjoyed both subjects.

My interest in geography led to my early interest in stamp collecting. The hobby got a big boost in the country by the publicity given to President Roosevelt's devotion to his stamp collection. When I became mobile again after my polio scare, with a few young friends I organized a stamp collectors' club. We met regularly around the dining room table in my home. We proudly showed off our recent acquisitions and did some swapping of extras. At one point, after we had contributed a couple of dollars to a pot, we answered an ad that offered two pounds of stamps from countries throughout the world for that amount. We placed the order, and when the bundle arrived we spent several sessions taking turns blindly selecting an item from the batch. The stamps had not been soaked but were still glued to pieces of envelope or package. We each had to spend a lot of time soaking our stamps and drying them on old newspapers. With many contributions of stamps from my father and several of his friends while he was still employed in New York City, and also regular contributions from my Grandma Darby of stamps from letters received from

Grandpa Darby's many relatives in England plus a few from her relatives in Germany, my foreign collection mounted in a big album grew to be quite respectable. I was so devoted to it that, when Aunt Nellie took my sister and me to New York City to visit Macy's and each select a Christmas present, I chose as my gift a particular set of Spanish stamps I had coveted. The trip also included attending the annual Christmas show at Rockefeller Center.

I continued my collecting of stamps into high school, but my collection remained untouched during my college and military years. When Betty and I moved to Buffalo, New York, on my job assignment for the Aetna Insurance Company, it was still among my possessions. When we found that Betty was pregnant with our first child, I took my albums to a stamp dealer in Buffalo and, probably foolishly, accepted his offer of three hundred dollars for the entire foreign collection. I retained my prized collection of U.S. stamps that was in a separate, very nice album I had received as a Christmas gift. Over the years, until Betty and I were ready to retire in 1984, I greatly enhanced my U.S. collection. At that time, I entrusted it to a philatelic auction company, and happily that collection fetched many times the amount I accepted for my foreign album.

Like my interest in geography, my interest in mathematics did not cease with the end of grade school. When my family moved from Mineola, I had to transfer to a grade school in Williston Park at the start of the eighth grade. Thus in a new environment I took the statewide tests required at that stage. I scored well in the one in mathematics as well as the others, resulting in my being selected as valedictorian of my new class. Less than a year later, when my mother, my sisters, and I moved again, and I became a student at East Hampton High School, my interest in mathematics really increased. A primary reason for this development was my exposure to a very enthusiastic and devoted math teacher. Mr. Miller was a forty-something-year-old bachelor whose only job since college had been teaching math courses at the high school. I came under his sway when I was a late arrival for his algebra class and rapidly caught up with my classmates. I particularly had his attention after I received the highest mark in the class on the State Regents examination at the end of the term.

Whereas many high school students felt that they'd had their fill of math after algebra, a fair number, mostly boys, opted to take Mr. Miller's plane geometry course the following year. Mr. Miller took great interest in the boys outside of the classroom as well as when teaching. On one occasion, he took five of us on a two-day trip to New York City to attend a burlesque show and see some sights. We all stayed at a YMCA where the fee was twenty-five cents a night. During the year, Mr. Miller decided that he would produce a minstrel show that would raise funds for school activities. Many boys spent a lot of afternoons after school learning skits and songs selected by Mr. Miller for the production. A good-sized crowd, including my mother and lots of other parents and students, crowded the auditorium on the night of the performance. My role was minor, and I was not one of the performers who wore blackface. At the conclusion of the term I miraculously achieved a perfect score on the State Regents test in geometry, a result for which Mr. Miller took full credit and broadcast throughout the town.

I had only been a member of Mr. Miller's advanced algebra class for a couple of weeks when I transferred from East Hampton High to John Marshall High School in Rochester, New York. At Marshall, the principal concluded that it would be impossible for me to join one of the math classes, so I ended up joining, as the only male, a typing class. The subject served me well at many times in my later life.

When I began college at the University of Rochester as a freshman in 1942, I was required to take two courses in the group classified as physical sciences, which included mathematics, chemistry, and physics. The group also included geology, and the dean who interviewed about my application for admission recommended that I opt for geology and Math I. I did not know at the time that he taught the geology course. Particularly in view of the turmoil of the wartime 1942–43 college year, they were good choices, since I found the geology course interesting and the math course not too challenging. However, since I entered the army at the end of my freshman year, the result was that I took no really challenging courses involving numbers from the time I left East Hampton until I returned to the U of R in 1946.

When I resumed my college studies, I was torn regarding my major area of study. Prior to service I had been a political science major, but some of my activities during service had led me to be equally interested in business courses and literature. When the same dean again interviewed me, he was most understanding regarding my dilemma. In addition to declaring me a junior based on credits for my various activities while in the army and air corps, he approved me enrolling for the ensuing term in two courses each in political science, English, and business administration. Our understanding was that, after auditing the courses, I would drop one to stay within the college rule limiting a student to five courses each term. By the end of the first testing period I was actively participating in, enjoying, and receiving high grades in each of the six courses and did not desire to drop any of them. The dean allowed an exception to the rule.

One of the two courses in business administration was Introductory Accounting. I was intrigued by the concept of being accurate when dealing with figures. I had become a very small-scale accountant while in the service by developing my own system of recording every penny I received or spent and doing a monthly account. My several small account books also contained listings of every book I had read and every movie I had seen during the almost three-year period. My accounting professor, who was also the chairman of the department, followed the college sports teams and obviously was aware that I was on the football squad. He also became aware in the spring that I was dating a cute former army nurse, since I introduced Betty to him when she and I attended a U of R basketball game and bumped into him upon entering the Palestra. I think I also got his attention when he assigned a long accounting problem as a take-home exam. I turned in my worksheets with two pennies taped to them. I had run out of time and my accounts were out of balance by two cents. He clearly did not hold my frivolity against me, as a year later he offered to recommend me for a teaching fellowship in the Business Administration Department at the University of Hawaii. Betty and I were then married and reluctantly decided that was not our desired future course.

My short career at the Aetna Insurance Company involved much dealing with numbers. The ten-week course I took at the company's headquarters in Hartford included not only introduction to the terms of the various insurance policies sold by the company but also training to assist agents in developing full insurance plans for small and large businesses. Developing an "Aetna Plan" required preparing a financial statement for the account involved. During my short term at the Aetna office in Buffalo, my boss considered me the office's Aetna Plan expert and assigned me to develop several studies for businesses not in the territory I was assigned to cover.

I had no occasion to become involved with accounting matters during law school. Similarly, neither during my second tour of duty in the army at Fort Eustis nor during my year as law clerk to Justice Stanley Reed at the U.S. Supreme Court from 1953 to 1954, was the subject of accounting of significance. It was not very long, however, after I departed Washington and began my legal practice in New Haven, Connecticut, that I began to be frequently involved in accounting matters. My field was litigation, and many trial matters involve at least a modicum of accounting. My first significant matter involving accounting, however, was when I was requested by one of the firm's senior partners to attempt to assist the president of a large local bank with a problem he was experiencing. The issue involved suspected improper activities by a number of tellers in handling their accounts. The subject was particularly touchy since the bank employed on a part-time basis a number of Yale students, including several from the Divinity School. I quietly investigated the matter by reviewing bank practices and interviewing many employees, and I submitted a carefully written report to the president. My report, which regretfully sustained some of the worst suspicions, enabled the president and the directors to remedy the problem without any adverse publicity. Only a short time later, the bank president contacted me again and requested me to look into his concern that a young vice president was committing fraud in the handling of bank loans. Once again I investigated and submitted a detailed report that, sadly, again verified the president's concern. The matter was referred by the bank to the federal prosecutor, and the vice president was indicted, tried, and found guilty. I really was not pleased when I was called as a prosecution witness in the case. I was pleased, though, when, as a result of my relation with the president, I was invited at a young age to become a member of the bank's board of trustees in 1958.

My second significant legal matter directly involving accounting was an action I brought on behalf of a large client of another of the senior partners. It was on behalf of a construction contractor, and the action was against the sole supplier of a vital material to the contractor. I brought the action under the price discrimination provisions of the federal Robinson-Patman Act. The claim was based primarily on an accounting study developed as a result of discovery proceedings. The claim was vigorously resisted, but our client prevailed in both the district court and when the judgment was appealed to the federal court of appeals.

My deep involvement in accounting matters expanded greatly when I left my legal practice and shortly became president and CEO of the area's electric utility company, United Illuminating Company. I assumed the position just as the electric companies in New England were experiencing a number of major crises. The Arab oil embargo of 1973 had caused a huge increase in the price of the fuel used in many of the region's generating plants, and a resulting skyrocketing in customers' electric bills and problems regarding the cost and feasibility of nuclear power plants being constructed to reduce the region's reliance on oil was causing turmoil in the financial markets, jeopardizing the continued construction of such units. As a consequence of these crises, I spent a major portion of my time preparing repetitive rate case presentations for the Connecticut rate regulators and meeting with financial institutions, politicians, the other owners and the builders of the nuclear plants regarding keeping those projects alive.

Since my company had not had a rate case proceeding for decades before these crises, the long-term chief financial officer of the company was unequipped and too intimidated to be the company's advocate, so the role fell to me. Even after I was successful in hiring a recent Harvard Business School graduate with strong accounting skills to assume the job of chief financial officer, the regulatory commissioners always requested my presence at the hearings to elucidate the facts and figures.

I quickly gained a reputation at the company for carefully studying every proposed budget or expenditure request. I also carefully studied each financial report prepared by the company's CPA firm. When I raised questions with that firm's partner assigned to the account about various entries, and actually found one significant error in the allocation of a charge, I acquired a reputation as a client for whom it was necessary to be able to explain and justify all accounting practices.

During my years as CEO of the electric company, I agreed to serve as a director on the boards of several other corporations headquartered in Connecticut. In every case, within a short time, I found myself appointed a member of each board's finance committee. That involved deeper review of the corporation's financial matters on behalf of the entire board.

My most interesting involvement during the period in accounting occurred when I was approached by the director of the Connecticut Public Expenditure Council, an organization funded and supported by the chamber of commerce and other business organizations. He invited me to become a member of the committee overseeing council activities. The director and his staff were charged with reviewing and analyzing all aspects of the state's financial operation. As chairman of that committee from 1978 to 1981, along with the director I met on a number of occasions with the governor to discuss the council's analyses of aspects of the state's finances.

Impressed by the detailed financial statements prepared by the company's CPAs for inclusion in annual reports to stockholders and regulatory agencies, I began preparing a set of personal financials each year emulating those of the company some years before I retired. Added to the journal I had maintained since my army days, I adopted monthly income and expense charts, a cash-flow chart, and an annual balance sheet with supporting schedules. Among the supporting schedules are detailed data regarding Betty's and my investments in stocks, bonds, mutual funds, and insurance policies. The sources for all of the schedules are account books that are always maintained on a current basis. I enjoyed being so organized, but Betty kidded me about my fixation with my accounting. I believe she considered it a manifestation of my Scottish heritage. Even before we were married, Betty enjoyed joking that I had misrepresented myself when we met as a French lover, when I was really a Scotsman.

Even in retirement, I could not escape involvement in accounting. During the first year after Betty and I moved to our condo in Point Brittany, I was elected treasurer of the condo owner's association for our building. In that capacity, it was my responsibility to prepare the annual budget for our building, which determined the monthly fee of owners. For many years my predecessors had accepted without questioning proposed budgets prepared by the accoun-tants for the managers of the six buildings that made up the community. When I reviewed the accountants' proposal, I questioned several items, including primarily a large charge for insurance cost on utilities in the individual units, since all owners already insured themselves. To resolve my dispute with the accountants about the propriety of the charge, I filed a formal request for a ruling with the state agency that regulated the huge number of condominiums in Florida. In due course, the agency issued a formal ruling sustaining my argu-ment, and I became a hero to all of the condo owners' groups.

When Betty and I moved to Croasdaile Village Retirement Home in North Carolina in 1999, I was sure I was through with finance committees. I was wrong. Within a year I was requested to serve on a residents' finance commit-tee, which met monthly with the executive director to assist in developing the annual budget for the home. At the outset, the home was managed exclusively by the executive director and a committee comprising leaders of the Meth-odist Church, which had founded the home. Various financing and financial problems about which they had limited experience led within a short time to that committee recognizing that they needed expert assistance. As a consequence, the committee contracted with Life Care Services (LCS), the manager of many such facilities throughout the country, to supervise the management of Croasdaile Village. When the executive director had the financial director from LCS address the residents' finance committee to present their plans, I engaged in a debate with him about LCS's proposed handling of Croasdaile Village's large bonded debt resulting from construction of the home. Based on my painful experience dealing with my company's experience financing nuclear plants, I made some suggestions regarding modifications of LCS's plans. Without acknowledgment, the most significant of my suggestions—a prompt refinancing of a high-rate bond issue—was accomplished.

Except for maintaining my own records, my involvement with numbers was thus ended.

My mother Irene Darby Fassett

Yale Law Professor Ralph S. Brown

Supreme Court Justice Stanley Reed

Attorney Frank Callahan

CHAPTER 4

Mentors

A lot of individuals have significantly influenced my life, but few of them would qualify as mentors. Webster defines a mentor as "a trusted counselor or guide." Can a mother qualify as a mentor to her child? As a former teacher, like many good teachers, my mother probably served as mentor to some of her students. But one does not ordinarily think of a parent in the same way as a mentor. However, to some extent, because of uncommon occurrences in my childhood, my mother was indeed my mentor as well as a loving parent. When I was largely confined to my bed and bedroom for what would have been my third-grade year in elementary school, I had no nursing or other care other than from my mother, and she made it a full-time occupation. While the teacher from my missed class dutifully prepared and sent reading and other materials so that I could attempt to keep up with my classmates, it fell to my mother to ensure that I did the work and, most importantly, that I thoroughly understood the work that was assigned. Mother taught me to be diligent and persevering. I came to welcome the additional assignments she offered based on her experience as a third-grade teacher in Lindenhurst, Long Island, and at Kew Gardens School in New York City. She and my father, another teacher and coach, had to change schools after they wed, since at that time the public school system would not employ a married woman as a teacher.

When I returned to school after one year (but not to rejoin my classmates since the administration decided that I was sufficiently advanced to skip a

33

grade), the routine that had been established during my incapacity essentially continued with my mother assisting with my studying. The routine became especially true when my parents moved to a different town and I entered a new school. Fitting into a new group apparently again proved a problem for the administration; once again, I skipped half a grade to become a member of the eighth-grade class at Park Avenue School in Williston Park, which graduated in January 1939. Although I was at least two years younger than all of my new classmates, I performed well in classes, was selected to be on the team representing the school in the regional spelling bee, and became valedictorian of the class based on Regents exams required by New York State for all eighth-graders. My mother quizzed me nightly from a long list of likely words before the spelling bee, and I am sure she was disappointed when I did not make the next stage. When I was told to draft a valedictory address, I labored diligently, but it did not become presentable until much editing from my mother. My teacher was much impressed with the product, and all went well at the graduation ceremony until my mind suddenly went blank at mid-oration. My mother, teacher, and the rest of the audience—including my grandparents, who were in attendance—were kept in suspense until my mind finally cleared and I resumed telling them about the upcoming World's Fair of 1939 to be held in Flushing Meadows, less than thirty miles from our school.

I had several other excellent teachers during my elementary and high school years who encouraged and inspired me, but none who actually qualified as a mentor. The closest candidate during my year and a quarter at East Hampton High School was not a classroom teacher but our physical education instructor and football coach. He was a recent graduate of my father's alma mater, Colgate University, and very gung ho. As I was a newcomer in 1940—only fourteen years old and not particularly big—I wouldn't have considered trying out for the high school football squad had not Coach Jones strongly urged me to do so. He had inherited a squad of only about fifteen players from his predecessor, who had moved to another school, and he needed quite a few recruits even to have an intersquad scrimmage. Coach Jones was enthusiastic, and he made the practice sessions every day after classes exhilarating and fun. Fortunately, he did not lose his enthusiasm when we did not have a winning season. We did win half of our games, almost entirely due to the performance of two of our veterans, the DiGate brothers, who played quarterback and fullback. After the end of the season, the coach assisted the older brother, a senior, in obtaining a full scholarship to a military school, where he could get more experience for a possible college career. During the summer of 1941 Coach Jones and his young bride both worked at a youth camp in upstate New York, and every week that summer each of us on the squad received a mimeographed sheet consisting partially of some educational material about the rules of football, but, in fact, largely a pep talk about the coming season. The coach's enthusiasm created a happy squad, but my happiness evaporated just prior to the first game of our 1941 season when my mother told me we were about to move again, this time to Rochester, New York, where my father had begun employment with the Allstate Insurance Company and had rented a nice house for us there. Recognizing my dejection, Coach Jones visited my mother and made a determined pitch for her to allow me to stay in East Hampton until I completed my senior year. He not only proposed that I live with him and his wife in their apartment near the school, but suggested that, if things went well, he would sponsor me for a football scholarship to Colgate University upon graduation. My mother rejected the proposal since she did not want to separate the family again. Nevertheless, Coach Jones did use his influence to have Colgate contact me about a possible scholarship.

My one candidate as a mentor when I started classes in midterm at John Marshall High School in Rochester was my homeroom and English teacher, Miss Foley. She was an older and obviously very experienced teacher, but she apparently felt considerable compassion for the young man who was thrust into an alien environment after the start of his senior year. She strongly encouraged me to contribute to discussions both in class and in homeroom. However, her primary mentoring activity involved encouraging me to write. Apparently she had for many years been a contributor to a teachers' organization publication, and she obviously submitted some of my musings to their annual compendium of student work, since I later received a copy of the volume containing my lengthy poem titled "Meditations." I believe Miss Foley also conspired with my history teacher, also elderly and very experienced, who was the coach of the school debating team, to get me included on the group even though I had no prior experience. Joining that group for meets with a few of the other high schools in Rochester constituted my only extracurricular activity while at John Marshall. I did not attend the senior prom, and one of my regrets is that I embarrassingly declined when a girl on the debate team invited me to be her prom date. Instead of joining my new classmates that night, two new friends and I rode around town, including around the country club where the dance was being held.

I had no one during my interrupted college years or during my two tours of military service who remotely qualified as a mentor. However, in both periods in the military I did have for an extended period an officer to whom I was assigned and with whom I worked closely who influenced my life significantly. While stationed at Douglas Air Force Base in Arizona in 1945 as a sergeant instructing candidates for a proposed Chinese Air Force in the basics of instrument navigation, I met Major Kubiak by happenstance. I spent a lot of my spare time in the Link Trainer building where I normally worked, since it was one of the few air-conditioned buildings on the base. One day the major, having survived fifty missions as the pilot of a heavy bomber in Europe and assigned to Douglas to await further orders, came to the building and requested a test flight on a Link Trainer. I happily accommodated him, we conversed, and it became a regular routine for the remainder of his short stay at Douglas for him to visit me for a session on my Link. The major was a business graduate of UCLA. With victory having been achieved in Europe and hopefully not too far off in the Pacific, he was awaiting orders to join a team for a project to undertake the closing—mothballing—of some air force bases that were becoming surplus. Other members of the project were assigned to engineering tasks dealing with disposition of buildings and equipment. Major Kubiak's role on the team was to be the disposition of personnel, and his personal specialty was to deal with officers. He told me that the Western Flying Training Command in San Antonio, Texas, which controlled all of the bases in the western states, was going to assign the other members of his team, but if I had the right qualifications, he was sure they would accept his recommendation to include me on his small team. As I related in my memoir, I did acquire the necessary qualifications, was included on his team, and for the final six months of my air corps career at Minter Field in Bakersfield and Mather Field in Sacramento, California, I supervised the disposition of enlisted personnel. My contacts with the major were much restricted after the commencement of the project due to our differences in rank. Most of my orders came by TWX from San Antonio, but he did oversee my performance. Early in 1946, when I advised him that I desperately wished to return and complete college, he signed the order that transferred me to Marysville, California, to be discharged.

My pseudo-mentor during my recall to service at the outset of the Korean conflict (I had been granted a commission as a second lieutenant as an administrative specialist after my earlier service) was also a major, but Major Reagan was much older than Major Kubiak. Having completed just one year at Yale Law School and being an unattached reservist, I was included on the order calling up the Railway Operating Battalion sponsored by the New Haven Railroad to fill an open position as administrative officer with such responsibilities as mess and supply. I didn't last even two weeks in that position after the unit arrived at Fort Eustis, Virginia, the training center for the Army Transportation Corps. Thanks to the recommendation of the unit's executive officer who knew I was a law student and knew people in the headquarters at the training center, I was promptly assigned to be assistant defense counsel on a general court-martial scheduled to be tried on the base. My performance in that capacity brought me to the attention of the commandant of the training center and resulted in my transfer to his staff and assignment to the small Courts and Boards Legal Section.

The Legal Section was headed by an elderly Tennessean who had served during World War I and later returned to school and been admitted to the

Tennessee bar. After practicing for some years, he obtained a commission and served during World War II and then opted for a regular army career. He was actually overdue for retirement. Prior to the Korean mobilization, he had an easy existence at Fort Eustis with few demands and two career master sergeants, one who doubled as the court stenographer, attending to virtually all limited activities of the office. During peacetime, courts-martial were extremely rare, and Major Reagan was able to spend most of his afternoons napping in the easy chair in his office.

With mobilization and the inundation of Fort Eustis by several railroad battalions and a large number of trucking and stevedoring companies, activity in the Legal Office rapidly increased. Prior to my assignment, junior officers from the various peacetime units had been assigned as prosecutors and defense counsel when the commandant ordered a court-martial. I became permanent prosecutor, but defense counsel were still assigned from the unit of the person charged. Prior to my assignment, the Legal Office performed few functions other than the trials, but with mobilization there was a proliferation of requests for reports, which I rapidly produced. When the commandant learned that lectures should be given to all officers and enlisted men about the new Code of Military Justice enacted by Congress in 1950, he directed me to undertake the task personally. The commandant also directed that I be issued a sidearm so that I would be properly armed while accompanying him on inspections or military reviews, which were becoming more frequent.

Major Reagan and I developed a very friendly relationship. He recommended a rental unit apartment very close to his in Newport News so that I was able to bring my pregnant wife and daughter, Joy, to join me. Betty and the major's wife became friends, and she was of great assistance to Betty in accommodating to life as an army wife.

The bottom line is that, while not a mentor, Major Reagan was a confidant and significantly influenced my life. Actually, the commandant, a colonel, whom I saw only occasionally, probably had more influence on my thinking. He was responsible for my being promoted to first lieutenant after only six months of active duty in grade. He tried vigorously to convince me to convert to a regular army commission and make the service my career. However, when I convinced him that my desperate desire was to return to law school, he took the steps necessary to expedite my release from active duty, so I missed only one year at Yale.

While I had been impressed by a couple of my first-year law school professors, none came close to being a mentor to me. The situation was essentially the same upon my return from the army during most of my second year, until the midpoint in the second term. I had never taken a course from Professor Ralph Brown, whose forte was intellectual property law, and I was surprised when I received a note in my cubicle stating that he would like to talk to me. I promptly made an appointment, and he informed me that he was embarking on a research project to produce a book for which he required an assistant and the dean had recommended me to him. The subject was to be loyalty programs in the United States, a subject then much in the news, with Senator Joe McCarthy's accusations often in the headlines. The project sounded intriguing to me, and I was prepared to accept an offer of the job even before Ralph proposed that I be paid two dollars an hour—double the normal student assistant rate. His grant would permit that expenditure.

Though technically Ralph might have qualified as my mentor for the period of more than a year I worked with him, we became good friends and, in fact, closer to being collaborators. When he suggested an aspect of the issue that required investigation, I would spend such time as I could spare from my classwork and away from Armoryville in the big, main Yale Library or in the smaller law school library until I felt I had exhausted the available sources. I would then write a summary of my findings and conclusions, attaching copies of my main sources so that he could decide if more work was necessary.

I was most pleasantly surprised, in fact astonished, when Ralph converted one of my first research memos into an article ("Loyalty Tests for Admission to the Bar") and submitted it to the *University of Chicago Law Review*, where it was published in 1953 with Ralph and myself as coauthors. Later in the same year, another coauthored article, titled "Security Tests for Maritime Workers: Due Process under the Port Security Program," was submitted by Ralph to the *Yale Law Journal* and published there. I had been elected to the board of the *Yale Law Journal* based on my class standing at the end of my first year, but had been neglecting all responsibilities there due to my military break and my work for Ralph since my return. That fact, plus that I was getting well-paid and credited with coauthorship of articles, was not popular with all of the students slaving to produce the issues of the *Yale Law Journal*. Ralph generously agreed to let me use some of the research that I had done for him to satisfy a part of my obligation to the *Journal*. Thus, though not published under my name, a third part of my research appeared in another 1953 issue of the *Journal*, titled "Loyalty and Private Employment: The Right of Employers to Discharge Suspected Subversives."

During the summer following completion of my second law-school year and prior to the publication of our articles, Ralph and I collaborated on an entirely different project. Ralph and his wife, also Betty, resided in a beautiful modern home overlooking Long Island Sound in Guilford, Connecticut. They had two very active young daughters and had not taken a vacation together for some years. We had visited the Browns' home socially a couple of times, so they had met my Betty and our two youngsters. The idea of getting away from the summer heat in our Quonset was attractive, and Betty bravely agreed to undertake overseeing four children at the shore so that the Browns could take a trip. Betty Brown made arrangements for their pediatrician to be available if needed, but no problems arose and the interlude flew by pleasantly for all.

I was not a party to the final production of Ralph's treatise titled *Loyalty and Security: Employment Tests in the United States* since it was not published by Yale University Press until 1958. I left the project after my graduation and promptly sat for the Connecticut bar exam since Justice Reed had requested that I arrive for my clerkship for the 1953 term of the Supreme Court as soon as feasible. Professor Brown did recognize me and a couple of other Yale students in the treatise as research assistants for the project.

My fourteen months (June 1953 to August 1954) as "head clerk" to Justice Reed—he used the adjective when hiring me and when he introduced me to the new chief justice, but I don't think it had any other significance, although I believe my compensation was a bit higher than a clerk hired directly from law school due to my years of military service—really should not qualify as an experience in which I was mentored. They more closely resembled the collaboration and friendship I had with Ralph Brown (though, of course, I was never credited as a coauthor of any of the issued opinions that emerged from my drafts). I have written at length about my roles during the term as an assistant and provocateur in several publications of the Supreme Court Historical Society and my lengthy biography of Justice Reed published in 1994 (*New Deal Justice: The Life of Stanley Reed of Kentucky*). The bottom line is that, although it was not really a mentoring experience, my work at the Supreme Court was the defining experience of my entire professional life.

When I left Washington and began practicing law in New Haven, I started the only true extended mentoring period of my life. I began almost immediately working with Frank Callahan, one of the four founding partners of the firm, and the only lawyer in the firm who devoted most of his time to litigation. Another partner, Fred Wiggin, had once been respected as a litigator, but he was quite elderly and had been essentially retired for a number of years. Two of the younger partners had tried some nonjury estate, taxation, and condemnation cases, but they had no interest in becoming trial lawyers. Frank showed me the ropes and supported me through the years. Frank's largest litigation client was the Liberty Mutual Insurance Company. It wrote a lot of liability policies in Connecticut and regularly referred files to Frank involving suits from automobile and other types of accidents that its claims representatives had been unsuccessful in settling. Most of the lawsuits were brought in state courts, but a few were also commenced in the federal district court, which also was located in New Haven. I spent much of my time and effort during my first few years at Wiggin & Dana drafting opinion letters to be signed by Frank summarizing the facts and issues and making recommendations regarding the disposition of literally hundreds of such cases. In the few cases that proceeded to trial, I accompanied Frank to the court involved and listened as the trial judge invariably made an effort, usually successful, to convince the plaintiff's lawyer to accept an offered settlement as soon as a jury had been impaneled. A few of those lawyers were notorious for never settling until that point because their contingency fee agreement with their client increased their percentage from 25 percent to 33⅓ percent at that stage. I recall only one case where I accompanied Frank to court and the case went to a jury verdict. Frank was an impressive-looking counselor in his early sixties (he had served as an able seaman on a naval vessel during World War I) with white hair, a bow tie, and a persuasive delivery style.

Frank would sometimes discuss my opinion letters with me before signing them, and he began inviting me to join him and two of the other founding partners for lunch a few times each week primarily to discuss client matters. After not too many months, Frank sent me to the Superior Court with a file involving a suit by one of the leading local plaintiffs' lawyers with instructions to dispose of it. It was a typical auto collision case in which the plaintiff had run up large medical bills for back treatments and claimed permanent disability. Egged on by the Liberty Mutual claims supervisor who attended the proceedings, and knowing that the head of the orthopedic department at Yale Medical School was quite willing to refute most of this plaintiff's claims, somewhat to the surprise of the trial judge who was a friend of Frank's and knew I was a novice at jury trials, I defended the case as a phony claim and argued to the jury for a complete rejection of it. To the dismay of the plaintiff and her lawyer, but to my great satisfaction, after only a couple of hours of deliberation, the jury returned a verdict for the defendant. That verdict made my reputation with Frank and the trial bar, and for a number of years thereafter I did virtually all of the liability trial work for the firm.

While both of Frank's lunching partners, Huntington Day and Arnon Thomas, got me involved early on in interesting activities for their corporate clients, I am sure that Frank was primarily responsible for my being made a partner in the firm as of January 1, 1958. Day represented several of the banks in town, and he assigned me to two interesting investigations involving malfeasance by tellers and fraud by a young officer at New Haven Savings Bank. My investigations, which also resulted in my becoming a prosecution witness in a criminal trial in the federal court, brought me into much contact with the president of the bank and resulted in him inviting me to become a member of the bank's board of trustees. Thomas represented the Register Publishing Company, publisher of New Haven's two daily newspapers. The company was controlled by a trust set up by the founder of the papers, John Day Jackson. Arnon asked me to join him as a co-trustee to help mediate the constant feuding among the Jackson heirs, particularly the two brothers who served as publisher and business manager of the publishing company. In due course I became a social friend with both of the brothers. Ultimately, as counsel to and a member of the board of directors of the Register Publishing Co., I handled some very interesting litigation.

After I became a partner and had gained some experience as both a trial and appellate lawyer, Frank and I began trying together a number of larger litigation matters first referred to us by Liberty Mutual, but later coming directly from some of Liberty's clients. By far the largest of these clients was United Aircraft Company (UAC), the biggest employer in Connecticut, with plants at several locations in the state. The first case was a suit against both National Airlines and UAC and alleged that a crash of a National flight was caused by a malfunction of a propeller manufactured by UAC's Hamilton Standard Division. Our client provided us with a massive investigation file, which I studied diligently, and I spent a number of days at home while recovering from a nasty case of adult chicken pox becoming an expert on the operation of our client's propellers. I became convinced of UAC's assertion that the fatal occurrence was caused by modifications made to the propeller by National's mechanics during maintenance, and an Ivy League engineering professor retained by UAC as an expert witness agreed. The case never went to trial, because after considering our defense, counsel for the plaintiffs settled with the airline.

The second case referred to us by UAC involved a helicopter manufactured by its Sikorsky division. A suit had been brought in the federal court by an ambitious attorney hoping to open a gold mine. It alleged that the deaths of several military personnel killed when a naval helicopter crashed in the water near Sasebo, Japan, were the result of a defective chain drive. Aside from the absence of precedent for actions by military personnel under such circumstances, the case raised many interesting legal questions. The initial one that intrigued me was the question of what law should be applicable in such a case. During discovery, plaintiff's counsel first asserted that he relied on the wrongful-death statutes of the American states of origin of those deceased; he argued alternatively that the federal Death on the High Seas Act should be applied. At a preliminary hearing on the issue of applicable law I had a Yale geography professor testify as an expert witness that the point of the accident was in the waters of the enclosed harbor of Sasebo, which definitely would not qualify as high seas. Without ever opining on the issue of any possible liability in such a situation, the federal judge held that, even if there could be liability in such a case, the only applicable law would be that of Japan, which did not allow damages in such circumstances. The case died.

Undoubtedly as a result of the contacts we had with UAC in those and a few other cases, in 1960, when UAC was being threatened with work stoppages at all of its plants by the labor union representing its employees, UAC's labor counsel from New York City telephoned Frank and retained our firm to represent the company in any litigation resulting from a strike. A long, bitter, and sometimes violent strike ensued, involving primarily the Sikorsky and Pratt and Whitney plants. There were times at the outset of the strike when Frank and I were both on trial at the same time before different judges in different counties seeking injunctions against mass picketing, violence against employees who sought to work, and even violence against the homes of some nonstrikers. After the strike ended, we initiated a legal action against the offending union for damages caused by illegal activities of the union during the strike. Frank was being assisted by one of our new associates when that hotly contested case reached trial in the superior court in Hartford. In the midst of one of the first days of trial, Frank collapsed in the courtroom and died. His demise, of course, ended our mentoring relationship. To add a footnote, I inherited the trial of the case that went on for many weeks and resulted in appeals both to the state supreme court and the U.S. Supreme Court attempting unsuccessfully to overturn the multimillion-dollar judgment rendered by the trial judge.

Not only did I sorely miss my relationship with Frank as I assumed the role of head of litigation at our firm, but I abruptly found myself in an entirely new position as mentor to a series of young lawyers.

Exelon Corporation
P.O. Box 805398
Chicago, Illinois 60680-5398

John W. Rowe
Chairman and
Chief Executive Officer

February 15, 2010

Mr. John D. Fassett
2600 Croasdaile Farm Parkway
Apartment 354
Durham NC 27705-1331

Dear Jack:

I returned from a wonderful vacation in India to find the unexpected delight of your
letter. We have not seen or corresponded in many years and I greatly appreciate your
taking the initiative. Needless to say I consider the work we did together on
Seabrook the formative process of my long career as a utility CEO. I have been
blessed with many opportunities, not the least of which has been to survive the
constant issues that plague our industry. Strange as it may seem, I am now the
"dean" of the industry, with 26 years as a CEO putting me well ahead of Jim Rogers
at about 21. Still I am viewed by many as a bit odd, due to the nature of the
companies I have run.

Your advice to me when I was frankly a lad is still remembered with great fondness.
You took me aside, early in my CMP days, and said, "given UI's problems, you may
not want any advice from me but I am going to offer it anyway. If I could change
one thing I have done, it would not involve Seabrook, a subject where I had few
choices, but rather I would replace more people faster with those who have more
energy and newer ideas." I have not always been able to follow that advice but have
always tried. You were a great gentleman and a fine utility executive who played a
very difficult hand with grace. What more can be said of any of us.

The issues of our business remain troubling. There is no honestly kept regulatory
model. Competition has many virtues but is always cheated upon. The Nation needs
more nuclear plants but they are not economic with today's gas prices. I have made
money for various shareholders and kept the lights on but it is hard to find many
tracks in energy policy.

Best to you and your wife. I hope retirement is good. I will try it soon enough my
self.

Sincerely,

CHAPTER 5

And Mentoring

Even before Frank Callahan and I had become entangled in all of the litigation emanating from the UAC strike, I was fast becoming overwhelmed by new business and I obviously needed assistance. In 1957 my partners readily agreed to an expansion of the litigation department, and with several of them I interviewed a recent graduate of the Yale Law School recommended to us by the president of Yale, Kingman Brewster. Brewster had met Joe Lieberman as the result of an article Joe wrote about a political dynasty in Connecticut. That subject probably should have been a warning to me about Joe's real interest, but, for a couple of years, Joe, as an associate at our firm, did a lot of research for me and for a few other partners and accompanied me to a number of hearings on motions and to a few trials.

After my successful results in the National Airlines and Sasebo cases, I continued to receive interesting referrals from UAC that I chose to handle myself. Two of those cases also involved helicopter crashes, one off the coast of Georgia and the other in Greenland. I engaged in a lot of discovery and preliminary motions in both of them, but neither proceeded to trial. I somewhat regretted when the Greenland suit was dropped since people at UAC had suggested that they might take me to Greenland to examine the crash scene. Another case did proceed to a federal court decision and an appeal to the Second Circuit Court. It involved an employee suing the Pratt & Whitney Division of UAC for alleged malpractice by its medical department in failing to diagnose the employee's lung disease during a routine physical examination. The plaintiff's well-known lawyer, Bill Zeman, had succeeded in a prior similar action, and he relied on that precedent when I filed a motion to dismiss the action. I argued that the plaintiff's only right, if any, based on an employer's doctor's misinterpretation of an X-ray film was pursuant to Connecticut's workmen's compensation statute. When the district judge before whom I was arguing my motion inquired about the precedent relied on by plaintiff, I dogmatically stated the case had been wrongly decided. To my great satisfaction and the amazement of the plaintiff's attorney, the judge agreed and so did a unanimous panel of the Second Circuit when we argued the appeal at the Federal Courthouse in Foley Square in New York City. It was my first appearance before that court.

The next interesting case I received from UAC received a lot more coverage in the press, but it fizzled out much faster. The action was brought on behalf of a number of tobacco farmers in the Connecticut River Valley (the upper river area was known for the production of high-quality leaf for cigar making) who asserted that the testing of jet engines at the Pratt & Whitney plant in East Hartford was the cause of a disease that blighted their crops. A number of studies were done for UAC refuting this claim, and the plaintiffs had no reputable support for their position. The case was dismissed by a superior court judge, and his decision was not even appealed.

While I tried to get Joe Lieberman interested in taking responsibility for handling my growing backlog of liability files, he had little interest in assuming such responsibility. Betty and I really liked Joe and his wife, whom we entertained and conversed with about the firm and his future. He had fast become engrossed in various aspects of New Haven politics, and it was apparent to me that his ambitions were in that direction rather than in becoming a partner in the firm. During a break between my court engagements, he and I had a long and convivial discussion during which I advised him that he had to choose whether he wanted to be a good lawyer or an active politician. Joe decided to leave Wiggin & Dana, and I am happy to acknowledge, in due course, that he became a prominent, able, and important political figure.

Happily for me, not long after Joe's departure, my concern about my need for assistance was greatly reduced as a result of a telephone call I received from a partner at a big New York law firm who had clerked for Justice Clark while I was clerking for Justice Reed. My clerkship friend told me that a young, married, and able Fordham Law School graduate had been employed by his firm for several years and was well liked by the partners for whom he worked. However, he disliked living and working in New York City and really aspired to a future in someplace like Connecticut, where his wife had grown up. Bill Egan came to New Haven for an interview with me and one of my partners, and based on my recommendation we offered him a position as an associate, which he promptly accepted. His hiring was a milestone of sorts for Wiggin & Dana since, except for one graduate each from Columbia and Harvard Law Schools (both of whose wives had deep roots in New Haven), every other associate and all of the firm's partners were graduates of Yale Law School.

Bill worked closely with me on the liability cases, and within a couple of years he was known and respected by the judges and beginning to handle such matters entirely on his own. In addition to the cases from UAC on which I received assistance from Bob Jelley, the associate who had been with Frank Callahan when he died in Hartford and had worked closely with me the remaining many weeks of my completion of the suit against the UAC union, I began to establish relationships with a few young lawyers not from our firm. In part due to contacts from other former Supreme Court law clerks who practiced in New York City and in part due to my having successfully tried several antitrust matters on behalf of clients—the opinions from which had been published in the *Federal Reporter*—I had begun to receive personal referrals of legal matters from a couple of large New York firms. Two of my early antitrust cases had involved criminal actions alleging violations of price-fixing statutes by manufacturers of rubber products and copper tubes. The most widely reported decision, however, was by District Court Judge Timbers in an action I had brought on behalf of one of Arnon Thomas's clients against Texaco for violation of the Robinson-Patman Act for price discrimination in the sale of asphalt. Judge Timbers had formerly been general counsel at the Securities and Exchange Commission, and he wrote a long, erudite, and to some extent groundbreaking opinion for my client resulting in a substantial settlement of the action.

Possibly as a result of the Texaco decision, but maybe as a result of my long employment interview with John W. Davis in 1952 before I had heard from Justice Reed regarding my clerkship at the Supreme Court, I was contacted by a partner in the large Davis Polk firm and asked if I would be willing to serve as local counsel in a Robinson-Patman Act class action case brought in the Connecticut Federal Court involving one of their large clients, United Fruit Company. At the opening of the first preliminary hearing in the case, I introduced the senior litigating partner from Davis Polk and his young associate to the federal judge, and they were admitted to practice for the case. However, after a couple of sessions, the partner obviously became satisfied with my taking the lead role in the case. He assigned his associate, Tom Griesa, to stay in New Haven to assist me, and although I conversed with the senior partner by phone frequently, I did not see him again during the very long trial. Not until the appeal of the very detailed findings entered by the trial judge (following a draft prepared by my new assistant and me, which the judge had requested) and entry of a final judgment in favor of the banana grower, importer, and seller to the Court of Appeals for the Second Circuit in New York City did I see the senior partner again. While the name of Davis Polk preceded that of Wiggin & Dana on the appellate brief, once again my very senior companion left the oral argument entirely to me. I was much relieved when our client prevailed again.

The lengthy discovery proceedings in the banana case and the actual trial to the court without a jury took quite a few weeks, and during that time I got to know my eager temporary associate very well. Since he was staying in a local hotel during the week, he was particularly able to spend long hours in my office, and he carefully fulfilled all of my requests for drafts of possible findings and all nature of other related research projects. At the end of the trial, Tom acknowledged that it had been a really enjoyable learning experience—quite unlike any he had yet experienced at his firm in the city. My curiosity about Tom Griesa's future course (I usually learned who had been made new partners in the big New York firms every year) was answered several years later when he was appointed by the president and confirmed by the Senate to a vacancy on the district court for the Southern District of New York. Just recently I read that a groundbreaking opinion he had written on an issue of international financial law had been affirmed by the U.S. Supreme Court.

Angus Gordon, one of Wiggin & Dana's younger partners, but older than me by seven years, worked primarily for one of the firm's largest corporate client, United Illuminating Company (UI), the electric company for southern Connecticut. Initially, Angus asked me to write an opinion letter regarding the possible merits of a legal action by the company against various suppliers of transformers for violations of the Sherman Antitrust Act.

When UI's directors voted to join a group of utilities considering a class action in the federal court in New York City, I was designated to represent our client in the proceedings. I had the pleasure—after a lot of preparation, meetings with lawyers for other utility companies, and negotiations with counsel for the defendants—to present to UI's directors a settlement check for in excess of a million dollars. The antitrust suit was just the first of a large number of other legal matters I handled by myself for UI. I also represented UI when a group of fishermen in Bridgeport sued the company for destroying their businesses when it constructed a generating station in the harbor. Other suits where I represented UI included when it was sued again when the same generator malfunctioned and soot was emitted over an area of the city, regarding a long-standing dispute with the New Haven Railroad about its charges for use of railway support structures for UI's transmission lines, and in two important actions involving permissions to construct new transmission lines from a new generating station on New Haven Harbor to the north and from the rail line to the western part of New Haven County. Several of these matters happened after Angus left Wiggin & Dana to become president of UI. They were a prelude to my becoming so deeply involved in utility affairs that I, too, after first becoming a board member of UI, left Wiggin & Dana and my trial practice and became vice president and general counsel of UI in 1973.

Perhaps I should have included Angus in my essay about mentors since I never worked closer with anyone than I did with him during my tumultuous first twelve months at UI. With crises related to the Arab oil embargo, the construction of generating stations, the formation of the New England Power Pool (NEPOOL), and politicians with respect to escalating electric rates due to soaring fuel cost, it was a very frustrating period. As a result, Angus decided to retire as CEO of the company as of September 1, 1974, and dogmatically refused to be swayed from his decision. At his recommendation, the board elected me president of the company.

While I developed close working relationships with several young engineers in UI's planning and operating departments and with a young lady in its financial department who rapidly produced computerized reports for me as I requested, the closest thing I had to a mentorship during this period was not with an employee. The first actual mentorship arose out of my representation of UI on the NEPOOL Executive Committee, where I became close friends with several CEOs of other New England electric companies, including New England Electric System (NEES), headquartered in Westboro, Massachusetts. At a time when I was virtually residing in Boston or Westboro while trying to deal with the threat to the regional power system due to the Arab oil embargo, the CEO of NEES assigned one of his young lawyers, John Rowe, to provide me with any assistance I might request. He worked closely with me, and later, when a crisis developed with respect to the construction of the Seabrook nuclear plant of which both UI and NEES were partial joint owners, John again became my assistant and protégé. The Seabrook crisis was twofold: first, antinuclear groups and some New England politicians were strongly opposing construction for varying reasons; second, as a result of the escalating cost of the project, the lead participant, Public Service of New Hampshire, had gone into receivership and abandoned its role. I had to step in and take control of the project, which meant having frequent meetings with bankers and other financial people and frequent meetings with political leaders in New England, particularly with Governor Sununu of New Hampshire. I also had weekly meetings at an office I had acquired in Boston with the joint owners and with the construction contractor to adopt a construction budget for each ensuing week, an unheard-of procedure in the industry. John accompanied me on most of these occasions and was available to perform any analysis or other task I requested. I am sure he was also keeping his boss at NEES fully informed of my activities, and I did not regret that such a conduit existed since I sorely needed strong support from NEES at critical junctures in the process of rescuing the project.

Happily, after much sweat and turmoil, the Seabrook project was financed and completed. Since it commenced operation in 1985, it has been one of the most dependable units on the NEPOOL grid. The young lawyer who was my helper throughout my last days in the electric business soon left NEES for an executive position with a midwestern utility. In due course, John Rowe became the CEO of one of the largest electric systems in the country, Exelon Corporation in Chicago. In 2011 I was thrilled to receive a note from him reminiscing about our time together. Among his comments were the following:

> Needless to say I consider the work we did together on Seabrook the formative process of my long career as a utility CEO.... Your advice to me when I was frankly a lad is still remembered with great fondness. You took me aside early in my CMP days, and said, "Given UI's problems, you may not want any advice from me but I am going to offer it anyway. If I could change one thing I have done, it would not involve Seabrook, a subject where I had few choices, but rather I would replace more people faster for

those who have more energy and new ideas." I have not always
been able to follow that advice but have always tried.

The other nonemployee of UI who came under my wing during my active
career at UI was an employee of the Register Publishing Company, where I
continued to serve as a director until the conflicts between the often-in-the-
news electric business and the newspaper business led me to resign from the
Register board. While still on that board, I offered some criticisms about what
I considered to be very slanted coverage of issues regarding electric companies.
The editor in chief responded that he really had nobody on his staff with any
understanding of the electric industry, and thus it was not very surprising that
most of the information reported was derived from politicians, environmen-
tal activists, or others with an axe to grind. The publisher inquired whether I
would have my staff at UI cooperate to help balance the knowledge of some of
their staff. I agreed to cooperate, and my newly elected assistant vice president
for communications, Anne (the first female officer in the investor-owned
utility industry), undertook the task and scheduled several seminar-type sessions for Register personnel.

Shortly after those sessions, Anne advised me that the editor had contacted her again because they had recently hired a bright young college graduate
who aspired to be a business reporter and requested that Anne confer with
him. Particularly because I recognized the new reporter's name, I stated that
I would meet personally with David Wessel and attempt to contribute to his
understanding of current energy issues and the issues of business generally.
David and I had at least three relaxed, hour-long discussions reposing in easy
chairs in my office during the following weeks. David also telephoned me a
few times with specific questions in the months prior to my retirement, but I
lost track of his career until I began to see financial articles in the *Wall Street
Journal* under his byline. In due course, David had moved to Washington for
the *Journal*, and he had a featured weekly commentary on economic subjects
titled "Capitol." I also began to see him as a guest on PBS's *Washington Week*

in Review on Friday evenings. He also became director of the Hutchins Center on Fiscal and Monetary Policy at the Brookings Institution. I swell with pride having known the distinguished economist as a cub reporter in New Haven— and feel grateful that I had a role in his early development as a journalist.

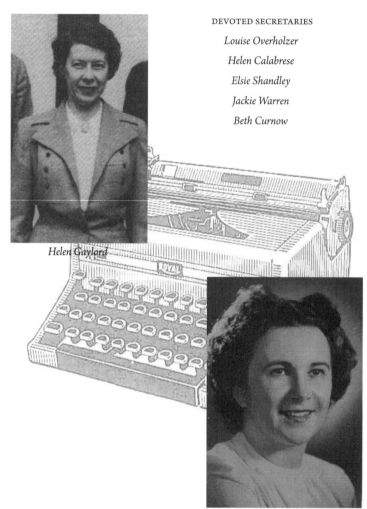

DEVOTED SECRETARIES

Louise Overholzer

Helen Calabrese

Elsie Shandley

Jackie Warren

Beth Curnow

Helen Gaylord

Clare Campbell

CHAPTER 6

Devoted Secretaries

I wonder if the advent of sophisticated computers, other new recording devices, and other revolutionary changes in the modern business and professional worlds have completely eliminated the role of the dedicated personal secretary. Maybe the remnants of the important functions performed by personal secretaries are now performed by "executive assistants" or some other such title, and I strongly suspect the persons employed with those titles are no longer all female, just as many of the bosses these days are not all males. However, during my youth and working career, personal secretaries, all female, were very important people. A number of them significantly impacted my life.

My first exposure to a personal secretary occurred when I was a young lad still wearing short pants. At the time of the 1929 crash initiating the Great Depression of the 1930s, my father was commuting to New York City from our home in Mineola on Long Island each weekday on the Long Island Rail Road. When my parents purchased their new house in a Mineola development, he was busily engaged as a broker of farm real estate with American Farm Realty Company, which had offices in the Chrysler Building. The company's owner had recruited my father to this position from his previous work as a high school teacher and part-time real estate agent in the farm country of southern New Jersey. Unfortunately, the real estate crash quickly followed the stock market crash, and American Farm Realty closed its doors. My father attempted to fight the tide in 1933 by opening his own office, Fassett Farm Agency, in the same building. He continued to commute regularly until it, too, went under in 1934, and he had to join the millions of unemployed men in this country.

While he was working at American Farm, I remember my parents talking about the able, middle-aged woman who served as his personal secretary. I got to meet Louise when she visited us in Mineola one weekend, and I recall that I always received a present from her on Christmas and my birthday. I still treasure a couple of the classic books she gave me. Louise continued with Dad when he opened his own company, but she also became unemployed when it closed its doors. Before that happened, I saw her on several Saturdays when my father took me to his office and I was assigned the task of folding and inserting in addressed envelopes detailed listings of available farm real estate that she had typed and my father had run off on a mimeograph machine. The business listed real estate not only in New York State and New Jersey but predominately on the Delmarva peninsula (Delaware, Maryland, and Virginia). On one occasion, my father took me with him while he made personal visits to his clients on that peninsula, and my strongest memory of that trip was being introduced at a dinner with one of those clients to French-fried potatoes with lots of catsup (tomatoes were the primary crop of the area).

Not until I had completed my first army tour and had graduated from college did I have occasion to meet another personal secretary who displayed the quality of loyalty of Louise. When I decided in early 1949 to sit for the new Law School Aptitude Test, which was being given in Buffalo, New York— where I was headquartered by my job with the Aetna Insurance Company, my employer since graduating from college in 1948—I was not entirely sure that I was prepared to spend three more years in school, especially since Betty and I were expecting our first child that summer. However, Betty and I discussed the matter at length, and she encouraged me to take the test—and if I did respectably, to apply to a couple of schools and see if I would be admitted. I still had a couple of years of GI Bill entitlement left, and she assured me that we would get by if necessary by her returning to nursing.

Having always performed well on tests, I was not entirely surprised when I received the results of the LSAT: I scored well, but I was amazed that I scored in the top percentile. In view of that result, I decided to apply to what to me were the two outstanding national law schools, Yale and Harvard. Within a few weeks I received letters from both schools asking me to contact them for personal interviews. The letter from Yale came from the secretary to the dean of the law school, and I decided to make that trip first because New Haven is close to Stamford, where my parents resided (avoiding the cost of a room), and because I knew it was much smaller than Harvard; I had heard some horror stories about the large classes and cutthroat competition in Cambridge.

My understanding boss allowed me to take a couple of days off to travel to Yale. although he couldn't understand why I would want to leave my current position (he opined that lawyers were "a dime a dozen"). When I arrived at the front, ground-floor office of the dean in the ornate, stone, block-square law school building on the north border of Yale's large downtown campus, I was met by his secretary/assistant and quickly introduced to him as he was about to rush off to teach a class. The rest of my visit was not rushed, as I spent several hours with Miss Campbell discussing my history and ambiguous aspirations. She seemed particularly interested in my diverse military experience (particularly my teaching of Chinese pilots) and was intrigued by Betty's role in the evacuation hospital unit accompanying General Patton's army at battles through Europe (particularly her award of battle stars for the Battles of the Bulge and Rhineland and their part in the liberation of Buchenwald). When I mentioned my concern about financing three more years of schooling, she stated that she could promise me fifteen hundred dollars in financial aid each year (half scholarship and half loan) if I attended Yale. When I responded that I was prepared to commit, she further amazed me by picking up her phone and calling the Yale Housing Office and obtaining a commitment of an apartment at 37 Hillhouse Avenue, a large former mansion near the campus that had been divided into ten apartments for veterans with children. She really smiled at our good fortune in finding an unassigned vacancy at 37 Hillhouse, since she had contemplated only the possibility of assuring me an apartment in one of the Quonset huts Yale had constructed adjacent to Yale Bowl to house married veterans.

To say that I was greatly impressed with the character, ability, and especially the initiative of the dean's secretary would be an understatement. I think I was grinning the whole trip back to Buffalo, and I couldn't wait to tell my pregnant wife (who worked her regular shift as a nurse in the obstetrics department at Buffalo Children's Hospital until the day our daughter was born) all of the good news. Of course, my second order of business upon arriving home was contacting Harvard and canceling my plan for a visit there.

I must add a footnote to this tale of the dean's dynamic secretary (not surprisingly, a couple of years later they became husband and wife). When I was doing research in the archives at the University of Kentucky in the early 1990s for the biography I was contemplating of Justice Stanley Reed, I found among his papers a copy of the letter sent by the dean in 1952 recommending me for a clerkship. It was a long, effusive letter, including references to both Betty's and my military experiences. Those references definitely confirmed for me that the letter had been drafted for the dean by his devoted secretary.

My next exposure to a most devoted secretary occurred as a result of that letter when I was selected as Justice Reed's clerk for the 1953 term of the U.S. Supreme Court. As he requested, I rushed to assume the position immediately after taking the Connecticut bar exam in mid-June 1953. The reason the justice wished me to expedite my arrival was that he had an appointment at Duke Medical Center for his annual physical and had plans immediately thereafter to depart for the summer at a cottage that the Reeds had rented in New York State near where their two sons resided. We literally had only a couple of hours of discussions before the justice departed. On my arrival at the court I also had to be sworn in (it was done both by the chief justice and by the court clerk), had to fill out a batch of papers for the clerk, and had to make arrangements with the marshal and security for a parking space in the garage below the court and for the identification badges and keys that I would require for my job.

The justice apparently had assumed that one of my predecessor 1952-term clerks would be available to orient me to my new position. However, that clerk had just been married and he couldn't wait to begin his honeymoon. Thus I had only a very cursory indoctrination from him, and my actual indoctrination was left to Justice Reed's longtime, very devoted secretary, Helen Gaylord. Helen and her older sister, Maggie, had come to Washington from mid-state New York as young ladies during the early days of the Depression looking for jobs.

Helen, having strong secretarial skills, was successful in finding employment at the Reconstruction Finance Corporation, a President Hoover creation that FDR retained. By coincidence, as a Kentucky lawyer who had actively represented a tobacco cooperative, Justice Reed also received his first Washington job at the RFC, and in due course Helen became his personal secretary. She followed him when he moved to the Department of Justice as solicitor general in 1935 and again when FDR appointed him to the Supreme Court in 1938.

Helen had not always enjoyed relationships with the justice's law clerks, but she and I immediately became friends. Having worked at the court for fifteen years and closely with the justice, she was an excellent teacher. Not only was she able to provide excellent advice regarding the justice's writing habits and likes and what he expected from a law clerk, but she also knew and was known by everybody in the marble palace. She took me on tours of the chambers of other justices and introduced me to their secretaries (most of the justices had departed promptly after the special session summoned by the chief justice dealing with the Rosenberg appeal) and some of their messengers. She took me on a tour of the impressive library and introduced me to the librarian and assistants whom I would have many occasions to rely on in the coming months. She also took me on a tour of other court facilities: the printers' shop, the cafeteria; the special area in the courtroom set aside for clerks or secretaries to enter and depart unobtrusively to observe oral arguments, even the barber shop.

The 1953 court term was, of course, destined to be one of the most momentous in our nation's history. Several appeals in the school segregation cases were scheduled to be reargued, but the momentousness was compounded by the fact that Chief Justice Vinson suddenly died on September 8 and President Eisenhower named Governor Earl Warren of California to succeed him. As related in *New Deal Justice* and in my memoir *The Shaping Years*, I became deeply involved in the segregation decisions with Justice Reed and also with the new chief justice. Throughout the busy term, I worked closely with Helen assisting the justice in work on *Brown v. Board of Education*, but also on his other significant opinions. When I developed a troublesome cyst of unknown origin on my body during the term, Helen insisted on calling her own doctor and getting an expedited appointment for me, resulting in the cyst being excised. Helen and I had become sufficiently close that, at the end of the term, after the Justice had again departed for Duke and his vacation and Betty and our kids had departed for Connecticut, I lived with Helen and Maggie in their nice Albemarle Road home until they took off for their annual Cape Cod vacation. Thereafter, I camped out in the justice's chambers for the few days necessary for me to complete my indoctrination of my successor head clerk.

The last time I saw Helen was in 1957. She telephoned to state that the justice desired to see me as soon as possible. The justice had retired from the court and was occupying a spacious office at the front of the courthouse, which overlooked the Capitol. President Eisenhower had just publicly announced his appointment of a commission on civil rights comprising prominent people and had named the justice as chairman. Helen offered to put me up when I came, and I, of course, promptly made arrangements for the trip. Since my eighteen-year-old daughter had not seen the court since she visited it as a toddler, I brought her along. We had a quick but very interesting visit with the Gaylord sisters and with the justice. He and I conversed for about an hour with my daughter and Helen quietly observing. He wished to discuss two aspects of his dilemma about his appointment with me: First, should he accept it or decline it? Second, if he did accept, would I come to Washington to accept the position of executive director? He advised me that Mrs. Reed opposed him taking the position, and as reported in *The Shaping Years*, "I frankly indicated grave reservations regarding the propriety of his serving on the Commission, and was very negative about my assuming any role with respect to it." History records that Justice Reed declined the appointment. My daughter remembers both her memorable visit to the court and our very pleasant visit with our hostesses in their house full of interesting antiques and beautiful cut glass (their father had been a glass cutter in the Corning Glass Factory in New York State) and when they served us fresh strawberries with our breakfast.

My next exposure to dedicated secretaries was even more personal. After Washington I became an associate at Wiggin & Dana, the largest law firm in New Haven. Betty and I had seriously considered my accepting positions at the Department of Justice and the Securities and Exchange Commission, but we questioned the desirability of raising children in the Washington area; then the offer from W&D to match my Supreme Court salary (considerably higher than the normal starting rate in Connecticut) closed the deal. (I also received renewed offers from Bob Taft when he visited the court to practice in Cincinnati and one delivered by a former Reed clerk to practice with a big firm in Cleveland that I had visited before I received the clerkship.)

By big-city standards, W&D was a very small firm when I arrived, consisting of four founding partners, three long-term associates, and three more recent associates. John Tilson, former Speaker of the House of Representatives, also occupied a prominent office in the complex, which consisted of individual offices of descending size for each of the lawyers, a small library (the County Bar Library was in the courthouse immediately across the street from the W&D offices), a small office for the bookkeeper/office manager, and a big room with many typewriters for the stenographic pool. Each of the founders had his personal secretary, but the rest of us had to depend on one of them if she wasn't busy or on one of the "floaters" or "temps" hired when the bookkeeper decided more help was needed. During my three years as an associate, most of my production was drafts of motions, briefs, and opinion letters produced by sharp pencil on pages from yellow legal pads. I could have produced some of my production by dictating on the Dictaphone machine the firm provided, but I did not like the instrument and never used it. My drafts of opinion letters were prepared for the signature of the senior litigation partner for whom I primarily worked, and his efficient secretary invariably typed them and saw to their execution and mailing. The balance of my production invariably was typed by the most senior partner's secretary. She obviously was not pressed for work, and she made no secret of the fact that she enjoyed doing my work. At the time, in addition to being an associate, I was also on the faculty at Yale as a visiting lecturer in the Political Science Department, and she happily reproduced for me various papers and tests I needed for my courses in constitutional law and history. Despite being overwhelmed by work during the period, I couldn't resist drafting a couple of chapters of a book I was contemplating writing about the Supreme Court, and she quickly volunteered to type them in her spare time.

As of January 1, 1958, the partners decided to promote me and the two other associates, who were also World War II vets and had been with the firm a couple of years longer than myself, to partnership status (but, of course, not partnership shares comparable to the founders or more senior partners). Our new status entitled us each to a personal secretary, and I went through the routine of interviewing several candidates whom our bookkeeper referred. I selected a slim, single, twenty-year old young lady who had graduated from secretarial school and proposed commuting to New Haven with her older sister from their home in Wallingford, a town between New Haven and Hartford. Coincidentally, my new secretary's name was Helen, and she became as devoted to her new role as Helen Gaylord had been to her position with Justice Reed.

Helen did all of my typing for over fourteen years. When I became the effective head of the litigation department as the result of my mentor's untimely death in the courtroom, she began helping with the drafts produced by several litigation associates we hired as the firm rapidly expanded in size. On many occasions Helen stayed long after the normal workday to complete a brief or motion that was due to be filed in court. That meant that she had to make connections for a long bus ride home, although on a few occasions when we finished work at the same time I drove her home before going to my home much nearer to New Haven. Helen's dedication was apparently the source of some teasing in the secretarial pool resulting (I learned much later) in several of the girls presenting her with a locket with my picture. It enormously embarrassed the deeply religious Catholic girl.

In 1973 I left the law firm and accepted the position of vice president and general counsel at the firm's largest client, United Illuminating Company. The change involved a move of only about five city blocks diagonally across the New Haven Green to the UI headquarters building. I had been doing a lot of legal work for UI for several years and had been elected to its board of directors in 1971. As an inducement to the position, I was provided, adjacent to the boardroom, a large office in which new shelves were built to accommodate my growing law library. A small room adjoined my office for my private secretary, and UI's chief executive officer offered to have the company employ Helen at an attractive salary if I desired to retain her in that position.

I offered Helen the option of moving with me and she eagerly accepted, but it turned out to be a big mistake. Instead of the stenographic pool she was alone in her little room adjacent to my office. My responsibilities representing UI on the executive committee of NEPOOL (the New England Power Exchange), on several other regional organizations, and on the legal committee of Edison Electric Institute took me out of town quite often, and she had no friends to converse or eat with. The situation was greatly exacerbated when, less than a year after our move, UI's president suddenly decided to retire and the board immediately elected me to that position. The move meant that I was moving to a more sumptuous suite of offices, but I was also inheriting an executive secretary who had spent her entire career at UI and had been personal secretary to prior presidents. Elsie knew everybody in the company and most of the officers, and managers relied on her when they had a question involving the executive offices.

Helen's and my problem was solved by my former partners agreeing to reemploy Helen at the firm, including reinstating her pension and other benefit plans, recognizing her prior service, but she weepingly yet happily departed the UI building and me. Elsie was not accustomed to having a boss who did a lot of dictating and also produced lots of pages of writing on yellow pages. I arranged for her to receive the first electric typewriter in the executive offices, and she loved it and found being kept busy was very satisfying. It didn't take very long for her to become an expert at deciphering my sometimes illegible handwriting, and she was scrupulous in assuring that I maintained my busy schedule. My one midweek relaxation during that period was a Wednesday noon tennis match against the young president of one of the local banks, and she enjoyed advising callers that I was not available because I was "in court." She really applauded my action when I appointed a longtime and conscientious employee in the Communications Department to be an assistant vice president, reportedly the first female officer in the investor-owned utility industry, and when a female professor from Yale Law School accepted my invitation to become a member of UI's board. The name "Elsie" acquired a dual meaning during my tenure because I adopted a program of awarding annually Elsies (I couldn't call them Oscars) to employees who performed some outstanding service for the company during the prior year.

When I accepted the position of president, I advised the board that it was on the condition that I be able to retire after a modest tenure since I wished to accomplish several other things in my life and I did not believe in lengthy executive tenures. In response to a question, I opined that eight years, the normal tenure for the nation's chief executives, seemed to be reasonable. As it turned out, I served well beyond eight years and did not retire until January 1, 1985, because a number of crises in the electric utility industry, particularly with respect to building and financing nuclear generators, delayed my exit. When it became clear that I was finally going to be able to occupy the retirement home I had built in Florida, Elsie, who had long been eligible based on years of service, filed her papers to retire on the same date. She told me that our years together were a crowning culmination to her long career.

Retirement did not completely divorce me from exposure to dedicated personal secretaries. I had recommended to my successor at UI for Elsie's position an able and efficient young lady in the company's accounting department who had accurately prepared for me on a number of occasions various charts and studies requested by state utility regulators. Jackie was enthusiastic in her new job, and shortly after my retirement while I was still a director and attended the monthly meetings of the board, my fellow directors suggested that I should write a history of the company. With the added urging of my successor, I agreed to undertake the project. I did my research each month while I was in New Haven in the company's archives and at the Yale Library and did the writing in sunny Florida. Jackie volunteered to type the many pages of draft I brought with me to the meeting each month, and she would then present me a carefully and accurately deciphered and proofread version of the prior month's draft. She took great pride in the project, and I couldn't have found a more pleasant collaborator on what was published in 1991 with the title UI: *History of an Electric Company—A Saga of Problems, Personalities, and Power Politics* (764 pages).

When I completed the UI book, I turned to a project that I had been delaying for over thirty years: a recounting of my experience at the Supreme Court. Initially, I submitted an article to the Supreme Court Historical Society, which it published in its 1986 Yearbook. While discussing the article with the SCHS editor, she strongly encouraged me to undertake production of a biography of Justice Reed, since his tenure on the court had been neglected while many of his contemporaries (particularly Justices Black and Douglas and Chief Justice Warren) had been remembered in multiple volumes.

My multiyear research and writing of the 771-page *New Deal Justice: The Life of Stanley Reed of Kentucky*, published in 1994, involved extensive research not only at Yale and in Kentucky, but at Stetson Law School, which was only a few miles from my home on Tierra Verde in Florida. The head librarian was very friendly and helpful (she was thrilled that a Supreme Court biography was being researched in her library), and when I fretted one day that I wished I had someone to assist me on this project as Jackie had on my UI book, she introduced me to Beth, the secretary for the *Stetson Law Review*. Beth had been typing drafts of articles for professors and students for some time, and she was enthusiastic at the idea of participating in the production of an actual book. Periodically, as I completed a draft of a chapter of my tome, I would bring the yellow pages to Beth, and within days I would pick up a carefully typed copy. After editing, I would return the copy to Beth, and it was rapidly transformed into a copy ready for the printer. I never knew when Beth did all of the typing, but I suspected most of it was done during evenings and weekends. She had always read and understood what she typed, and we sometimes had discussions about the contents. Beth was a worthy successor to Jackie, and I really regretted the end of my days as an author in Florida when I no longer had occasion to visit Stetson Law School and Beth.

I am sure that devoted personal secretaries of many other editors as well as of doctors, administrators, and other professionals in North Carolina as well as Florida with whom Betty and I dealt in the twenty years since *New Deal Justice* was published impacted Betty's and my lives, but none have stood out like the ones I have described. I certainly hope they are not part of an extinct profession!

Dr. Bob Hart and Rusty Hart, RN

Dr. Andy Wong and Irene Wong, RN

Dr. Andy Chau

CHAPTER 7

Me and the Medical Profession

As she had with my older sister eighteen months earlier, in January 1926 my mother traveled out on Long Island to her parents' home in East Hampton for my birth. I was delivered by Dr. David Edwards, the sole practitioner in the modest-sized town during the quiet winter months. As the site of many large summer houses of affluent mostly New Yorkers (although there were also clusters of people from other cities, including a significant Cincinnati colony), there were a few additional doctors living in the area during the season, but they were also vacationing and only available for their established patients during emergencies. The nearest hospital to East Hampton was in Southhampton, which was about twenty miles closer to New York City. Any major medical problem of any summer resident invariably meant being taken to a doctor or hospital in the city.

My mother also took my sister and me to have our tonsils removed, a medical ritual of that time, during an occasion shortly after we commenced school in Mineola. Dr. Edwards collected some ten or so of his young patients during a spring week in the assembly room at a local church where cots had been installed and a visiting surgeon removed tonsils on a production line. All of us were required to stay on our cots for a couple of days before being released to our families. I visited Dr. Edwards one other time in my youth when, while chopping wood in the back lot at my grandparents' home, I hit my leg with the axe and caused a nasty wound. Although it was Sunday, the doctor was waiting for us at his office (which was in the front of his house) in the center of town and quickly stitched and bandaged my wound.

My first medical experience at our home in Mineola occurred when I was only seven and my parents, concerned about the virtual epidemic of poliomyelitis in the country, took me to be checked out by doctors whose office was in the local hospital, a building only a couple of blocks from the Long Island Rail Road station. As a result of that visit and the resulting diagnosis, I spent most of the next year confined to my bed receiving various physical treatments, but no medications since none had yet been developed to treat polio. For many months I was not able to walk, and my mother had to carry me to and from the car to take me to periodic examinations by the doctors. I missed a year of school before I was deemed able to attend on my own, but rather than failing third grade, upon my returning, as a result of my having kept up with my classwork as well as having received much additional teaching from my former-teacher mother, I was deemed ready for fifth grade.

My other medical memories of Mineola involve a later visit to the hospital and my first recognition of the consequences of diseases and mortality. My mother went to the local hospital rather than to East Hampton for the birth of my younger sister in 1937. Unlike today, it was the custom for the mother and newborn to remain in the hospital for a minimum of ten days after birth. My sister and I were being cared for by a conscientious neighbor girl when our father was not home. However, we were concerned about our mother, so to alleviate our concerns, our father arranged to have our mother and new baby come to a window on the third floor of the hospital so that we could wave to her from the street below (children were not allowed as visitors in the hospital).

Unfortunately, I was not the only child deemed sick during the deep Depression years of our residence on Marcellus Road in Mineola. There were a lot of kids in the development whose fathers were daily commuters to jobs in New York City. I vividly remember a vivacious contemporary named Edith who was hospitalized, I was told, with some rare bone disease. When she was finally able to see her friends, I was shocked to see the awful, deep scars on both of her legs. Bruce lived on our block in a house between ours and Edith's. After he was absent from the games our gang played regularly out in the street, we were told that he had been found to have tuberculosis. Following medical advice, his family was moving to Arizona where he would have a better chance of recovery. Willy, like most of my classmates, was a couple of years older than I, and he lived on the next street in the development so he wasn't a regular member of our group. But when he suddenly died as a result of an infection from a cyst on his bottom, my mother decided to take me to the viewing in his home before the burial. It was my first experience with death and an important lesson. Not very long after Willy, the son of one of my mother's garden club friends also died, and she also took me to his viewing, but it involved a closed casket. She explained to me that he had been playing with matches and set himself on fire, causing his death. She emphasized the lesson of not playing with matches by describing how badly parts of his body had been burned. It was a memorable and revolting lesson.

My exposure to the medical profession expanded during our short period of residence in Williston Park after our Mineola house was repossessed by the FHA. Just as the Depression had begun to improve and my father was beginning to return to employment as a real estate agent, his health deteriorated precipitously. He was diagnosed as requiring surgery for a malfunctioning thyroid gland and admitted to Mineola Hospital. Surgery began, but was not completed due to his failing condition on the operating table; he was sent home to gain strength so that the operation could be completed. Thus, for several months he was essentially bedridden in our much smaller new house. During the same period, our grandmother suffered a serious heart attack and was similarly bedridden in East Hampton. As I became accustomed to a new school system, my mother juggled her weekdays, encouraging my father to prepare for his return to the hospital and commuting virtually all of her weekends to assist in caring for her mother (my very young sister accompanied her on those trips). As planned, my father did return to the hospital, and his thyroidectomy was supposedly successfully completed (I say "supposedly" since a few years later he was sent to Sloan Kettering Cancer Center in New York City and most of his cancerous esophagus was removed). Upon recuperating from completion of the thyroidectomy and with the national economy improving, he was able to begin employment as a route man for the Metropolitan Insurance Company, the job he had when my mother, my sisters, and I packed our belongings to move to our grandparents' residence in East Hampton to live with my grandfather after Grandma Darby had succumbed to another heart attack.

After those trying years, I had an interlude while I attended East Hampton High School and John Marshall High School in Rochester, New York, when I had no memorable contacts with the medical profession. However, in 1942, when I began college at the University of Rochester as a sixteen-year-old and succumbed to the invitation to try out for the freshman football team, I experienced one of my most memorable medical experiences. Although I weighed barely 150 pounds, I was fast and combative and had played on the high school team on Long Island. As a result, I was ultimately assigned to the first team on offense as a running guard on the T-formation and as a linebacker on defense. (In those days it was not uncommon for players to play on both the offensive and defensive squads.) The first two games of our season were against Manlius Military Academy and Morrisville Agricultural College, both two-year post–high school institutions. We played their varsities, both larger and older squads. As the *Rochester Democrat and Chronicle* reported the day after the Aggie game, our opponents "scored 28 points by application of brute force." At the outset of the second half I collided with Morrisville's fullback head on, and I played the remainder of the game with a bloody nose and not knowing where I was. Upon our return to our campus, Dr. Fauver, the athletics physician, had me admitted to the hospital where they treated my nose locally and released me on Monday with a prescription of epiphederine. However, before I returned to practice, Dr. Fauver and the trainer combined to develop a mask for my helmet, which I believe was the forerunner of the facial masks virtually all players wear today. Since mine was unique and there were not yet any rules against grabbing a mask, the first move of many of my opponents when I played guard was to grab my mask. In any event, the mask did not prevent me from having a nosebleed in every remaining game, and when the frosh scrimmaged the varsity in the traditional affair at the end of the season, the college paper reported that "the only bright thing on the field was Fassett's blood." Because of my breathing problem from my mashed nose, I failed the army physical when I took it toward the end of my freshman year, Dr. Fauver made arrangements for me to have surgery at the university hospital promptly after my last class, and after the swelling of my nose and my two black eyes improved, I was able to breathe adequately enough to pass the army physical and become a private on August 4, 1943.

My only two direct exposures to the medical profession between my enlistment and February 26, 1946, when I was discharged, were both brief. When I was sent to the Air Corps (it had not yet become the air force) Classification Center for aviation cadet evaluation in early 1944, the process included physical, visual, and psychological tests. Having been forewarned by a number of the members of the group preceding mine that the visual test would require one to be able to cross his eyes, I spent hours trying to accomplish that phenomena without much success and was much relieved when I, having already demonstrated sharp depth perception, was not requested to perform the act. The warnings we received about the psychological testing included tales of some weird inquiries about one's social and sexual history, but when I entered the office of the psychologist and saluted him (he was a captain), he immediately got up and shook my hand using what we called the Psi U grip. We then had a long discussion about our experiences as members of Psi Upsilon fraternity chapters at different universities.

My second military experience was with another branch of the medical profession, dentistry. It occurred during my air corps tour at Lowry Field in Denver, Colorado, as my company of graduating armorers was about to begin our training as gunners on flying fortresses. Studies had been done that showed that flying at high altitudes (B-17 crews flew on oxygen at twenty thousand feet or higher on bombing missions) caused severe toothaches for some crewmembers, especially those with wisdom teeth. The proposed solution was to extract all wisdom teeth before high-altitude training. Thus, one day our company was marched in formation to the base hospital, about a mile away on the other side of the field, where one by one we were admitted to dentists' chairs. Any existing wisdom teeth on the right side were extracted.

Two weeks later, we repeated the march and procedure and lost our left-side wisdom teeth. Those of us who suffered the extractions sure were envious of those classmates who were found not yet to have any wisdom teeth.

While I had only the two direct contacts with the medical profession during my first military tour, I actually spent quite a bit of time thinking and reading about medicine as a lifetime career. While I was stationed at Cornell University in the ASTP I had little spare time to think about postwar matters, but I did firmly conclude that I had no desire to become an engineer. When the air corps sent me to Biloxi, Mississippi; Stuttgart, Arkansas; Denver, Colorado; Douglas, Arizona; and Bakersfield and Sacramento, California, I mostly spent my free time carrying on extensive correspondence with family, former buddies, and many female acquaintances, one of whom, following a Rochester furlough, sent me a daily note in an envelope bearing heavy lipstick and SWAK for many months. We had been introduced by my parents' former neighbors. I also did a lot of reading when I could get my hands on decent material (everything published written by Dos Passos, Fitzgerald, Hemingway, Sandburg, Steinbeck, and Wolfe, and lots of lesser-known and foreign writers whose works had found their way into the generally disorganized small libraries maintained on military bases). However, more significantly, I did some reading and thinking about pursuing a postservice career in medicine. My experiences as an instructor and a personnel boss with a number of subordinates during my final months in the service taught me that I enjoyed dealing with people. Thinking perhaps that a medical field rather than political science should be my goal upon returning to college, I browsed a couple of medical treatises I found in a library and actually corresponded with my alma mater to determine what it would require to make me eligible for medical school. A quick study of the bulletin they sent me made it abundantly clear that a major alteration and probably an extension of my program would be necessary for me to stand any real chance of being admitted to medical school. As a result, I became reconciled to resuming my political science major upon my return to the U of R.

Between being selected by my fraternity brothers and the alumni to be manager of the Psi U house upon its return to us by the navy V12 in mid-1946 and my readily accepting an invitation by the coach to return to the football squad as well as undertaking a full schedule of courses, I was exceedingly busy during the fall term in 1946. In fact, I was so busy that on several occasions when my fraternity brother and fellow alumnus of the 1942 frosh team inquired whether I would like to meet a "cute nurse," I turned him down. My friend Ray had always been a premed major and had the good fortune of having been able to complete most of his medical school requirements while in service. Accordingly, in 1946 he was ready to commence med school at the U of R, but he ate most of his dinners at the Psi U house (much better than any of the cafeterias or college dining rooms). Finally, after the last game of the football season, I agreed to accompany Ray to a house near the women's campus (which was a half dozen miles from the men's campus) to have a double-date with the "cute nurse." Ray dated another cute nurse he had met in the final days of his service. Thus began for me an entirely different and extended association with a variety of aspects of the medical profession.

I should note that my final varsity football experience in the fall of 1946 was not as bloody as it had been my frosh career. I again played on the line on offense and as a linebacker on defense, but my nose, protected by an improved nose guard, went through the season without injury. I did get removed from one game long enough for the trainer to yank back in joint two fingers on my left hand that had been stepped on. Also, after the second game of the season, the doctor decided that my chest pains were caused by cracked ribs. He prescribed that my chest be taped. To my consternation, before he taped me, he had the trainer obtain a razor and proceed to shave my upper body of the chest hair of which I had been proud. Once it was removed, they taped me from my chest to my navel with heavy adhesive tape. As a result of being so immobilized, the coach decided not to include me on the trip to the following week's game at St. Lawrence University. However, I was included and played most of our next away game at the University of Vermont.

Betty (my "cute nurse") and Chick, Ray's date, had served together as nurses with an evacuation hospital unit attached to General Patton's Third Army. They had seen action in France, Belgium, and Germany. Their outfit had been awarded battle stars for both the Battle of the Bulge and the Battle of Rhineland, and they had seen the liberation of the Nazi concentration camp at Buchenwald and the meeting of American and Russian forces. Then, upon discharge, Betty and Chick both decided to pursue further nursing education, and possibly because Ray was heading back to the U of R, they chose to enroll in the course in nursing education offered by the U of R's Nursing Education Department.

From the time Betty and I became inseparable, which happened shortly after our first date and continued for sixty-seven years, virtually all of our closest friends were medical professionals: hers, as had been the case since she graduated from the Allegheny General Hospital School of Nursing in 1942, were nurses; mine, first future-doctor Ray and then, throughout my career, many practicing and teaching physicians with a variety of specialties.

Betty was the maid of honor when Chick and Ray were married at her home in New Hampshire in June 1947. Betty and I accompanied the newly-weds when they returned from their honeymoon in Boston and continued it for several weeks at a cottage on Lake Sunapee that her parents had rented for the occasion. Chick and Ray hurried back to Rochester for August 4 so that they could also participate in Betty's and my nuptial festivities. All of us were quite busy when classes resumed after Labor Day. We resided at opposite ends of Rochester, but we usually managed to keep Saturday night dates when we typically played bridge and drank a half gallon of Gallo wine with water until well into Sunday. On one memorable Saturday when we were playing at the Rapps' place, Ray suggested that I accompany him to his school while the girls prepared dinner. I had never visited the facilities of the medical school and was shocked when he took me to the room where the cadaver he was assigned to work with was. He removed the sheet covering the naked body and commenced showing the excisions he had performed. That brief experience spoiled my dinner that night and reconfirmed that such aspects of the medical profession were not for me. Ray loved surgery, and after medical school and several years of surgical residency at Syracuse Hospital, he and Chick moved to Berkeley, California, where he had a very successful abdominal surgical practice. Betty and I visited their Berkeley home overlooking San Francisco

Bay once, and they came east to visit us twice—once when we were in North Haven, Connecticut, and once when we were in Tierra Verde, Florida. Unfortunately, Ray died at an early age, and Chick followed not long thereafter.

After my graduation in 1948 there was a short interlude while I attended an insurance training course in Hartford, Connecticut, and Betty stayed with my parents in Stamford and worked at the Stamford Hospital. Betty and I thought we were settling down. We rented a spacious new garden apartment in Allenhurst Gardens in Amherst, a suburb of Buffalo where I had been assigned by the Aetna Insurance Company. Soon after we arrived, it became clear that we required the services of an OB-GYN, and my boss's wife recommended Dr. Hiram Yellen. The referral was most fortuitous for a couple of reasons. First, when we attended Betty's first appointment, it was like the reunion of Betty's Evacuation Hospital Unit I had attended with her, Chick, and Ray in 1947. As Colonel Yellen, he had been commanding officer of a different hospital unit in Europe during World War II, and he admired army nurses. He immediately called the head nurse at Children's Hospital, who had served in his unit, and arranged for Betty to be employed in the obstetrics section. He insisted that Betty should keep busy during the pregnancy. Since many of the women and babies Betty cared for during the next seven months were patients of Dr. Yellen, she saw him regularly, and she worked in her scrub gown until the day our daughter was born on August 5, 1949. When baby Joy was barely a month old and the three of us visited Dr. Yellen's office as we were about to leave for New Haven where I was to start law school, he lectured Betty about taking care of herself and the baby and lectured me about making sure they were both properly fed and cared for. He then refused to accept any payment for our outstanding bill, except for taking twenty dollars, which he immediately placed in Joy's wee hand.

Aside from Dr. Yellen I had no contacts with anyone in the medical profession except for Betty during our year in Amherst. I never met any of the doctors or nurses with whom Betty worked. However, fifty years later when Betty and I moved to the Croasdaile Village Retirement Home in Durham, North Carolina, I met Dr. Reckow, who with his wife also had recently moved in. He had been a pediatric resident in 1948–49 working at Children's Hospital.

Our only entertainment while we were in Amherst consisted of going out to a driving range where Betty would watch me erratically drive a couple of cans of golf balls. (I had been advised that a person in my job should be able to play golf with the agents I visited and, to encourage me, had been presented with a bag and a couple of clubs.) We also joined a couple of young neighbors on Friday nights to watch the fights on TV. On Saturday nights we watched Sid Caesar and Imogene Coca. Betty and I did not own a TV set of our own until five years later when we lived in Maryland.

Betty had lots of contacts with medical professionals after we moved to New Haven for me to attend law school in 1949. She shortly joined a nurses' registry and was regularly called about her availability to take private-duty assignments in the surgical recovery unit at Yale–New Haven Hospital. She worked only the 4–12 shift when I was free from classes and available to feed, change, and rock our daughter while I pored over law books. Usually, if Betty accepted an assignment, the case would last for five or six days until the patient was discharged from the hospital, but occasionally an assignment would continue for a number of weeks. The registry desired that the nurses on all three shifts would remain with an assigned patient until discharge, however long it involved. Most of Betty's cases were very challenging since she was usually assigned to neurosurgery cases, and many of them had received lobotomies, a treatment in vogue for a period for serious mental problems.

Since we were housed on the Yale campus and close to a bus stop for a short bus ride to the hospital, our location was convenient for Betty, but we both worried about her having to ride a bus home at midnight. (We had sold our car as soon as we arrived at Yale.) After a couple of months of that concern, Betty's routine was eased considerably when the husband of one of our neighbors offered to drive her home. The mansion in which we lived had been converted by Yale to ten apartments for married veterans with children. Our neighbor was a candidate for a doctorate in psychology. He was conducting an experiment using rats for his thesis, and he found that he had to take regular readings on his rats at midnight at his lab located in a building that was part of the hospital complex. Having a ride home from our neighbor rather than worrying about catching a bus at midnight made Betty's routine less worrisome for both of us.

I was lucky when I was recalled as an army lieutenant in June 1950, immediately after the commencement of the Korean conflict, that Betty and Joy were able to join me in Newport News, Virginia, where I found an apartment close to my base at Fort Eustis. I had been transferred from a transportation battalion to a position as legal officer on the staff of the training commander. In the course of my regular duty of prosecuting special courts-martial for the training command, I had occasion to cross-examine quite a few medical people. Often a soldier tried for stealing or being absent without leave would claim a medical excuse. The one case that I vividly recall involved a regular army sergeant being tried for self-maiming to avoid being deployed to Korea. The commandant strongly wished to nix the idea that such routine could be successful. During the trial, the defense counsel raised a defense of insanity and produced a psychiatrist who testified that the soldier must have been temporarily insane, since no sane person would stick his fingers under a bumper jack and sever parts of two of them. I had an interesting time probing the doctor's training and theory. The panel of officers spent very few minutes before returning a verdict of guilty. It was an interesting prelude to my years of examining various medical specialists during my career as a trial lawyer some years later.

Having become pregnant shortly after I received the telegram recalling me for military service, Betty's only medical activity at Fort Eustis consisted of monthly trips to the base hospital for examinations and her admission in mid-March 1951 for the delivery of our son. She was kept in the hospital for ten days after delivery. Joy was cared for by Daisy, a girl from Newport News we had hired to assist Betty, and Mrs. Reagan, the wife of Major Reagan, my superior in the legal section on the base and another near neighbor. Betty was not impressed by the quality of the medical service at the base hospital, but she was impressed with the fact that our total bill was only twelve dollars covering her food while in the hospital. She always suspected that the captain who delivered our son had been partying heavily in the officers' club when he was called for the delivery.

When we returned to Yale after only one year more of military duty, our convenient apartment on the campus was not available, so we were relegated to an apartment consisting of half of a Quonset hut in the large Quonset hut village that Yale had constructed near its armory and Yale Bowl several miles from the main campus. We decided to retain the Chevrolet I had purchased when I was recalled so that I could commute to law school classes and activities, and so that Betty could reactivate her listing on the nurses' registry. Known as Armoryville, the community consisted of about fifty Quonsets, each containing two apartments (each entering from an end at ground level). Armoryville housed grad students from various schools with their families, mostly including a couple of young children. It was a great place for Joy and Jack (they enjoyed bathing in the shower or the kitchen sink and did not mind sharing a minuscule room) since they had lots of playmates and an adjacent playground with swings, slides, and sandboxes. It was also a convenient place for Betty and me to discover many couples anxious to play bridge on those rare occasions when I was not studying and Betty was not working. When Betty was on a case at the hospital (she was still being called to tend neurosurgery patients), I would return with the car by three in the afternoon so that she could don her starched white uniform (which I would occasionally iron), pack her Velveeta cheese sandwich, and hasten to drive the few miles to the hospital so that she could arrive with adequate time to receive a full report from the nurse on the morning shift she was relieving. She splurged when she was working on Friday and got her dinner from the cafeteria since she liked their clam chowder.

Many of our neighbors in Armoryville were medical students or residents, and most of our new friends were from that group. Our most frequent bridge opponents consisted of a student who graduated from med school when I got my law degree in 1953 and his wife. They soon departed for Milwaukee where he was about to join a general practice. On those few occasions when we required a doctor during our two years in the confined and often uncomfortable Quonset (hot under the curved metal roof in the summer and unevenly heated by a coal stove in the winter), we were introduced to Dr. Wessel, who was willing to make house calls to the Quonsets. We came to know him better in later years when we settled in the New Haven area.

Instead of moving to Hartford, where I had accepted a position with a law firm and where Betty and I had closely examined the housing market with an emphasis on good schools for our growing children, when I graduated in 1953 we ended up moving to Silver Spring, Maryland. To my amazement and great pleasure, I was selected by Associate Justice Stanley Reed of the U.S. Supreme Court to be his law clerk for the court's ensuing term. We lived in another garden apartment development, which contained lots of youngsters for Joy and Jack to play with, but Betty's desire to resume nursing could not be satisfied since my job required me to depart before eight six mornings a week and I did not arrive home for Betty's and my dinner until about eight (the children were always fed and ready for bed when I arrived). We had no time for a social life except for the excitement in December when we received a formal invitation to and attended a reception and dinner at the White House with President Eisenhower and his wife, Mamie. The one other concession we made to entertainment was the purchase of a fourteen-inch TV set so that the children could watch the children's shows that were proliferating in the afternoons and early evenings.

Betty would have liked to do some nursing while we were in the Washington area, and she actually interviewed for a position at a retirement home near our apartment, but with my schedule it was not practical for her to accept any position. Our only other contact with the medical profession during our Washington year occurred in the spring when Joy developed a bad case of tonsillitis. The doctor who examined Joy decided that she required a tonsillectomy, and Betty chose to have her admitted to the Seventh-Day Adventist Hospital in Takoma Park since it was close to our home and it would let Betty stay in the hospital with Joy to nurse her. They had an interesting and successful experience, and Jack also had an interesting experience since I brought him to the court with me for the few days Joy and Betty were hospitalized.

Betty's and my long and deep associations with additional medical professionals really began when we moved back to Connecticut from Washington so that I could begin practice with the New Haven firm of Wiggin & Dana.

After a couple of weekends of exploration, we had agreed to purchase a house under construction in a small, seven-house development at the juncture of Ridge Road and Bishop Street in North Haven, a growing community with good schools (Joy was ready to start) adjacent to New Haven. Promptly after we moved into our almost finished but not yet landscaped house on Labor Day weekend, 1954, we promptly discovered that one of our neighbors, whose backyard abutted ours and who had three young children, was a practicing primary care physician. His wife, a graduate nurse, still substituted as his office nurse. Bob and Rusty Hart became our close friends. They remained among our closest friends for the rest of their lives.

At the outset, our relations with the Harts consisted mostly of conversations in our yards as we both got settled. Soon we developed a regular Wednesday night (early quitting time) bridge game, where we did almost as much talking as playing. Bob and I would discuss medical subjects, and he sometimes loaned me his *New England Journal of Medicine* so that I could read about some medical development. The Harts had previously been playing with another doctor, a pediatrician, also with a wife trained as a nurse, and we created a biweekly two-table Saturday night cocktails-and-bridge group by adding another lawyer and his wife. That group was soon expanded even further by adding another physician, an insurance agent, and an industrial engineer and their wives for full-fledged dinner parties on New Years' Eve and many other holidays. After a few years, with all of the Fassett and Hart children, we undertook a couple of camping trips together to state parks in Connecticut and Rhode Island, and one memorable Memorial Day weekend we all took off to explore Myrtle Beach in South Carolina.

In addition to his private practice, Bob had worked since completion of his residency at Yale Hospital at the large Veterans' Administration hospital in West Haven, Connecticut. While their children were still in elementary school, Bob was diagnosed with tuberculosis and himself admitted to the VA hospital (he had served in the navy during World War II), where a lobe of one of his lungs was removed. While he was there Rusty was diagnosed with the same disease and admitted to another institution for care. While Bob's mother came from

New Hampshire to live with the children, Betty and I became pseudo-parents particularly to the two boys. Fortunately, after a number of months, both Bob and Rusty were allowed to return to their home (and he to his practice) and our close relationship, although somewhat restricted, resumed. After a few years, our families went together for summer vacations on Nantucket Island, and when all of the children were older and away at school, we took a couple of weeklong winter vacations on islands in the Caribbean.

While Betty's and my social life in North Haven involved many contacts with doctors and nurses, my practice at Wiggin & Dana involved me even more with the area medical community. From my arrival at the firm I became a part of its small but very active litigation section. While I participated in (and later tried myself) some large antitrust, contract, and regulatory agency cases, most of my work even after I became a partner in 1958 involved defending negligence cases for insurance companies. The Liberty Mutual Insurance Company, which was a major Connecticut liability insurer, was an important client. Most of the suits involved automobile accidents (particularly collisions claiming serious back injuries) or falls on sidewalks or in business establishments. A few attorneys in the state brought most of the suits, and they invariably offered as their medical witness a New Haven neurosurgeon who regularly prescribed months of physical therapy (in his office) and often performed spinal operations, including laminectomies or fusions. Our clients usually retained the head of the neurosurgery department at Yale to review such claims. His opinion of those plaintiffs' attorneys and their doctor was not very high. Early in my trial career he recommended to me several medical treatises that I obtained, and we developed an ability to have informed discussions regarding the cases. Most of the cases were settled prior to trial (often immediately after selecting the jury)—partially because of pressure from the trial judge to settle and also because such attorneys were entitled to collect a higher fee then than by settling before the jury was selected. When a trial ensued, my expert, with his outstanding credentials, always was ready to testify for me, even though he loathed the necessity of having to participate in a trial.

In addition to the head of neurosurgery and the other surgeons in that department whom I came to know personally, I became acquainted with many other Yale doctors through my practice. My firm was well-known to all of them since it had represented Yale and the hospital for many years, and one of my partners taught a course on legal medicine at the medical school every year. Probably my greatest surprise from my doctor friends in New Haven occurred when my colleague and mentor from the neurosurgery department called one week and said that the local medical association (the New Haven County Medical Association, which owned a house near downtown where they maintained their offices and held their monthly dinner meetings) was having their monthly meeting the following evening and he would like me to come as his guest and meet some friends of his. I accepted, and when I arrived I was surprised to receive a round of applause and be advised that during the earlier business meeting I had been elected an honorary member of the association. Of course, I was astonished and pleased.

A few years after we moved to North Haven we ended up with another physician neighbor who moved into a nice new house a couple of blocks from ours. Bill Billings headed a three-doctor OB-GYN practice in New Haven, and while Bob Hart was our family doctor, Betty went to Bill's group for matters within their specialty. The Billingses had a second home on the Long Island Sound waterfront in Guilford, and Betty and I enjoyed a couple of swimming and informal dinner parties there. Bill consulted with me about a number of personal and business matters.

Right after school let out at the end of June 1962, Betty and I took off with Joy and Jackie on a camping trip to Acadia National Park in Maine, a tour around Nova Scotia, and a visit to Bay of Fundy National Park in New Brunswick. Although it rained throughout our tour of Nova Scotia, it was a great trip. Shortly after we returned, Betty and I learned that she was pregnant—somewhat of a surprise since she was approaching her forty-second birthday. Of course, this new situation required that Betty cut down on all of her many activities in our town; she had worked for many months for the Visiting Nurses Association, calling on residents needing nursing assistance, and she volunteered to work each month for the blood collection drive conducted by the Red Cross at the large Pratt & Whitney Aircraft manufacturing plant in the business area of town. As her pregnancy advanced, Betty was, of course, seen regularly by one of Dr. Billings's partners, and late on April 5, 1963, I called Bill and he directed me to take Betty directly to the hospital. He met us there, and after Betty was admitted to a room and prepped, he installed me on a cot in the doctors' room adjacent to the delivery room. Early in the morning I was summoned as Lora Jean was born and joined our happy family.

As Joy and Jack grew older and he went off to prep school and she left for college, Betty, Lora, and I spent more of our leisure time at the Lawn Club, an old New Haven institution with a very good dining room, eight well-kept clay tennis courts, an able teaching professional, exercise rooms, lockers, and showering facilities. I developed a schedule of a couple of evening matches each week, and Betty, Lora, and I commonly spent all of our Saturdays at the club. After a few lessons and a lot of practice with her junior group, Lora became a fine young tennis player. She and I won the annual parent-child tournament by defeating a prominent banker and his son in the finals one Saturday before an appreciative audience.

My favorite evening match, which involved us having to have a late dinner, was with a prominent young surgeon from the Yale–New Haven Hospital. Betty developed a friendship and playing partnership with a former nurse and wife of the head of the Ophthalmology Department at the hospital. Soon, her husband, Andy Wong, and I also became tennis partners, and in due course both partnerships made the Lawn Club team. The team annually played several other club teams from Connecticut plus an annual match against the Agawam Club from Massachusetts, where we played on grass courts rather than on clay. The year when it was our turn to travel to Agawam and be hosted at their famous club, Betty and I traveled with Andy and Irene. The four of us made up the senior contingent of our team. Our younger squad was enhanced by several strong players from Yale. Despite the grass, we narrowly prevailed and had a wonderful time.

After that pleasant affair, the Wongs often invited us to their very modern home in Hamden on Sleeping Giant (an area landmark). Sometimes we savored Irene's Hawaiian cooking. Other times we visited a busy local Italian restaurant where the owner welcomed us through the kitchen door and took us to a special table. It seemed that most everyone in town knew Andy; he had a great reputation for having successfully dealt with lots of people's eye problems. When I retired and Betty and I moved to Florida, on a number of occasions we stayed with and were entertained by the Wongs when visiting New Haven. We kept in contact until they both died, but we did not visit each other after Andy retired. They moved to Hawaii, where they both had grown up.

I sometimes regretted that I had not known Andy when Jack was a youngster. When Jack was tested upon starting school, he was found to lack vision in one eye. Another specialist diagnosed a juvenile cataract. He deemed it unwise to operate on it until Jack got much older, so for many years Betty went through the routine of taking Jack for a quarterly physician exam to monitor the cataract's development. He also required regular visits to an oculist to determine if any change was appropriate in his glasses. Not until he was a teenager on summer vacation was Jack hospitalized to have the cataract removed. Theoretically, he was not supposed to engage in any vigorous or contact sports because of his eye, but in fact he participated vigorously as a soccer player both in prep school and in college.

Luckily, Jack's eye problem was the only major medical problem our kids suffered in Connecticut, although they had their share of normal childhood accidents and maladies. Joy fell out of a tree and broke her arm and also suffered from mastoiditis and a ruptured eardrum. Lora developed an allergy problem that required a number of visits to a specialist, and we also had to rush her to a local surgeon one day when she got a prong from a Mister Potato Head embedded in her foot from stepping on it. She was very brave while the doctor removed the sharp plastic piece, but I started to faint while watching the procedure and was ejected to the waiting room. Betty commented, as she had on several other occasions when I became faint on observing bleeding, that the event reconfirmed that I never had any business thinking about becoming a doctor.

Dr. Wessel, whom we knew from Armoryville, did make some routine visits to our home for common childhood maladies, but mostly Bob Hart took care of the children as well as Betty and me. While we still lived on Bishop Street, Joy and Jack came down with chicken pox at the same time, but they did not get very sick and they recovered uneventfully. However, I soon also acquired the disease, and for me it was not uneventful; I ran high temperatures and was very sick for over two weeks. The timing of the illness could not have been more unfortunate, as I was in the midst of preparing to defend a major case in federal court involving an aircraft crash.

In 1973 I made a decision to leave the practice of law and become a corporate executive at the United Illuminating Company (UI). During that same year Betty and I sold our home on Bishop Street and moved to one on Old Orchard Road, a very attractive street nearer to New Haven, that Betty and I had long admired. We had even more medical profession neighbors on our new street than at our former home. Our house was on a corner, and directly across the street from our side yard resided Jack and Rosemary Haley. He was a pediatrician. Across the street from our front lived Bob and Mary Jordan. Bob practiced internal medicine and surgery, and their next-door neighbors were Dr. German, a psychiatrist at the medical school, and his wife. Neither Betty nor I had ever met Dr. German, but he had an eminent reputation. Dr. Jordan served as company doctor for my new electric utility employer, and I had just recently met him as he had performed the thorough exam I was given in connection with my employment. Jack and Rosemary Haley had in recent years become members of our holiday partying group. Old Orchard Road, named for the apple orchard that once covered the area (there were still old fruit trees in many yards, including two in our rear), was shaped like an L, and immediately at the turn resided two more physicians and their families, the Kashgarians and the Baskins. Dr. Kashgarian was a pathologist at the hospital, and his next-door neighbor was a urologist in private practice. The Kashgarians had two daughters, the younger of whom was a friend and classmate of Lora's at Ridge Road School, which she had recently started to attend, and later also at Choate where they went for high school. Dr. Baskin, the urologist whom I had consulted for a medical problem, was famous on the road for owning a large cider press that he would produce at harvest time each year so that there could be a pressing of most of the apples from the trees, culminating in a cider and dancing party. It was a pleasant neighborhood, and Betty and

I enjoyed our residence there until we bought a condo in Florida and I was preparing for retirement.

Aside from seeing new neighbors and old friends who were in various aspects of the medical profession, I had relatively few occasions during my dozen years heading United Illuminating Company to deal with medical issues. The two most major events that I recall involved burns and radiation. The first occurred a couple of years after I entered management. A bad accident occurred at one of our generating stations in Bridgeport when a huge quantity of scalding steam escaped from a generator and severely burned several employees. The local hospital was aware of the risk and had facilities to provide the best care possible to those involved. As a result of the incident and conversations with several of the medical personnel involved, I quickly agreed to have UI further endow the hospital facility and training of staff for such an emergency. My new awareness that Bridgeport as well as New Haven had an important medical community also led to my decision to propose appointment of an eminent Bridgeport physician to UI's board of directors when the next vacancy occurred.

The second medical event that confronted me while at UI (I exclude my own hospital bouts for operations for a ruptured hernia and for hemorrhoids, both of which were performed by Dr. Jordan) arose from my deep involvement with a consortium of New England utilities, including UI supporting construction of nuclear power plants. Much of the widespread opposition at the time was noisy, sometimes physical, often heated and political. I was involved in trying to respond rationally to all of those opponents. One other group I met with on several occasions especially troubled me. It consisted of medical and academic types who strongly argued that nuclear plants should not be constructed because they were too hazardous to human health. Desiring expert advice, I convinced Dr. Alan Bromley, head of the Physics Department and the nuclear lab at Yale, to join UI's board, and Alan and I became good friends. Alan was a very practical man, and he had trained at operating nuclear facilities in Canada before coming to Yale. He discussed frankly with me the dangers and benefits of nuclear generation, and I regretted to see him leave New Haven when he was named science advisor to President Reagan.

For the first ten years subsequent to Betty's and my retirement to sunny Florida in 1985, virtually all of our contacts with medical personnel were social. While Bob and Rusty Hart also shortly retired to Florida, he, of course, was no longer practicing, and they settled next to his brother about an hour away from us, so we naturally had to develop new relationships with a primary physician and a dermatologist (a requisite due to sun damage in Florida). Through our tennis playing at our local club, Betty and I both developed partnerships with medical people. Jean Milhauser, who became one of Betty's regular partners, had also been an army nurse during World War II. After playing a number of interclub matches with other partners, Andy Chau and I discovered each other, and we remained frequent partners as long as Betty and I remained in Florida. Andy had an intriguing history: he was born and received his basic academic and medical education in China, but came to this country as Mao was taking over China after World War II. He underwent more training and did several years of surgical residencies before becoming a prominent surgeon in Indiana; he married another doctor who also grew up in China, and they retired to Florida only a few months before Betty and I did.

During the first ten years of our retirement, my life centered around playing lots of tennis, working diligently to produce two heavy books and a couple of articles for publication, and commuting from Tampa to Connecticut for a couple of days each month to attend directors' meetings at UI and several other businesses that I had served for a number of years. Andy and I soon expanded from playing lots of club and interclub matches to playing in the seniors' tournaments that were scheduled at clubs in Florida throughout the winter months. Players over age sixty came from all over the country to play in these tournaments. Through the years we did respectably, although we never attained a national ranking (although I was so ranked in singles in 1989). However, Andy and I reached a high point when we were selected to represent Florida in the Senior Olympics at Syracuse University in upstate New York in July 1991. We got beat in the semifinals, but Loretta, Betty, Andy, and I had a great adventure living in a dormitory and marching into the Carrier Dome with other teams from throughout the country emulating the real Olympics. All our teammates dressed in orange shirts and white shorts. We were entertained royally.

Betty and I had a few medical emergencies before 1996. She tripped on a tennis ball on a court and fell and broke her wrist. I kicked a large bay catfish I had caught and ended up in the emergency room for removal of a sharp catfish spine from my foot and treatment for an exotic disease spread by such fish. Not until that year, however, did we become deeply involved with St. Petersburg's active medical community. In that year Betty was diagnosed by Dr. Cohen, a specialist at the hospital to whom we had been referred by our primary physician, as having chronic inflammatory demyelinating polyneuropathy (CIDP). She began receiving IV treatments with an expensive blood-derived serum at the hospital every couple of weeks. That was just the beginning of a series of health crises, culminating in Betty undergoing open-heart surgery for the removal of a large myxoma (tumor) in the left chamber of her heart in 1998. Andy Chau sat with me for the several hours while that unusual operation, especially for the St. Petersburg Hospital, was being performed by a team of surgeons and nurses. All of these maladies led to our move to Croasdaile Village Retirement Home in Durham, North Carolina, in 1999.

In North Carolina, Betty and I rapidly became acquainted with many different medical professionals both at our new home and at the renowned Duke Medical Center. Dr. Cohen's counterpart was Dr. Morganlander, who continued Betty's IV treatments for a period and then also referred us to Dr. Scott for treatment of an emerging case of Parkinsonism. For Betty's heart, Betty was initially seen by Dr. Cahliff, the director of cardiology at Duke, and as Betty had a sequence of serious heart problems including several emergency admissions to Duke Hospital, she was seen by many of the cardiologists on the Duke staff, including the specialists who inserted a pacemaker in her chest to monitor and control her heartbeat.

Dr. Heidi White, a geriatrician, was Betty's primary physician and has been mine since arriving at Croasdaile Village, and most examinations and routine matters have been handled by her staff in the Croasdaile clinic, consisting of two able nurse practitioners assisted by a nursing staff. To add to Betty's other woes, as a result of a mammogram performed in 2000, she was diagnosed with cancer in one of her breasts in 2000. A mastectomy was performed at Durham Regional Hospital. I had surgery in Duke Hospital by Dr. Bollinger for a double abdominal hernia the following year. Both Betty and I had operations for removal of cataracts performed by our ophthalmologist, Dr. McCracken, in a satellite Duke facility that handled such procedures. Betty had a number of stays in the nursing home pavilion at Croasdaile following her hospital visits and following falling episodes in the apartment. There she was attended by an efficient nursing staff and by Dr. White and a rotating cadre of young doctors on geriatric residencies.

Most of the foregoing occurrences are recounted in more detail in the volume titled *Betty: Chronicle of a Moving Life*, published by Chapel Hill Press in 2008.

CHAPTER 8

Sports

Amazingly, although my father was a high school basketball coach when he met my mother, a third-grade teacher, in Lindenhurst, Long Island, he never attempted to teach me to play basketball. During the school year before they were wed, my mother attended every game of the basketball team and recorded some of the details in her daily diary. When I saw the diary, I was surprised to learn that the winning team rarely scored as high as twenty points.

I did engage in some pickup baseball and kickball games in a sandlot a short way from our development house in Mineola. When Grandpa Fassett visited us and labored diligently to construct a two-car garage at the rear of our short driveway, he attached a peach basket minus its bottom above one of the doors, and all of the neighborhood kids took turns shooting baskets with a rubber ball about half the size of a basketball. I guess the reason my father never joined my sister and me in that pastime was, it being the depth of the Great Depression, that he was unemployed and working for the WPA and also in the early stages of the thyroid disease that resulted in two hospitalizations for surgery and kept him incapacitated for at least a year.

The only sport I ever played with my father was learning to hit a tennis ball. Just a couple of times he took my sister and me to a small Mineola park that had a fenced, hard-surfaced court with a net. From somewhere he produced a round-headed wooden tennis racquet and a can of old tennis balls, and my sister and I took turns trying to hit the balls to him over the net. Father gave me the racquet, and I still had it when I moved with my mother and sisters in 1940 to East Hampton, a small town located on the Atlantic Ocean near to the eastern end of Long Island. Living in East Hampton was not an entirely new experience to me since my sister and I had spent many happy weeks there every summer as we grew up. The lovely ocean beach was only three blocks from our grandparents' home, and we spent lots of afternoons enjoying the sand, swimming, and riding waves to shore. By the time I was twelve I had become a strong swimmer, and during our year as residents I acquired most of the skills of an ocean lifeguard.

During the spring of my first year as an East Hampton High School student, one of the teachers invited me and a few other boys to a meeting to discuss the idea of forming a high school tennis team. In the town park across the street from the school were two nice tennis courts where a couple of the boys had been engaging in games for several years. Coach Clark had played tennis in college, and he was successful in organizing and instructing a squad sufficiently competitive so that we were able to play matches against three other Suffolk County schools that year. I used my father's old wooden racquet.

As a result of my participation on that high school team, my tennis career blossomed. Needing a job for the summer of 1941, I took the advice of some friends and Grandpa Darby and signed on to be a caddy at the Maidstone Golf Club, the local club for the town's affluent summer residents. Shortly after first light each morning after school recessed for the summer in early June I began showing up at the caddy shack behind the pro shop at the club and joining a group of boys plus a number of older men who caddied for a living. I was both inexperienced and ignorant about the rules and etiquette of golf. The only preparation I received was a couple of lessons from a friend about the names and characteristics of the most common golf clubs.

The procedure each morning was for the caddymaster to call names to proceed to the first tee of the famous men's course to meet and pick up the bag of the player to whom one was assigned. Many of the men had regular or favorite caddies. In any event, unless the weather turned bad, all of the more experienced men and boys were called. Only on a couple of mornings did I have the experience of caddying with a male foursome. A round on the difficult course through dunes and across a pond as well as on the beautifully maintained long fairways and greens normally took at least three hours, for which a caddy could expect to receive two or three dollars, depending on the generosity and the mood of his player.

In addition to the men's course, Maidstone also had a shorter women's course with its first tee not very far from the other first tee. All of the holes on the women's course were designed to be less difficult than the championship course. After a couple of days of leaving the caddy shack and returning home without any income, the caddymaster told me I was assigned to a lady on the women's course since she decided she needed a caddy. Most of the ladies either carried or wheeled their own bags, which were much lighter and contained many fewer clubs while playing their more sociable golf rounds. My assignment was a charming younger lady who was a pretty good golfer, as were all in her foursome. However, they were all even better conversationalists. Her group did about as much chatting as they did golfing, and before eighteen holes were completed they had thoroughly interrogated me about life in East Hampton for a year-round resident, people and activities at the high school, and my life history. To my great pleasure, I received a three-dollar tip at the end of the round, which took equally as long as any round on the longer men's course.

When I returned to the caddy shack the following morning, the caddymaster told me I had been requested to caddy again for the same player. I was pleased—and even more pleased when, during the course of the round, I was asked how I would like to have a job at the Maidstone Tennis Club rather than being a caddy. My lady told me that, in addition to their golf games several mornings a week, her group played tennis several afternoons each week at the Tennis Club. Yesterday she had mentioned to the tennis pro that she had had a caddy that morning who played on the high school tennis team. I guess she gave me a good recommendation since he needed help to work in the men's locker room and perform other duties for the new season and said I should see him promptly. Coincidentally, the professional, who spent his winters as the pro at a club in Clearwater, Florida, had just asked his daughter, a classmate of my older sister at East Hampton High School, for the names of any classmates she knew who were interested in tennis. She lived with her mother, who had chosen to live year-round in town. My name was on her list.

I rode my bicycle directly from the Golf Club to the Tennis Club that day, a distance of a few miles, but much nearer to the Darby homestead than was the Golf Club. Before I arrived home for a very late lunch I had met with the tennis pro, who was just getting organized for the new season, and I had agreed to accept his job offer. The terms of the offer were that I would have responsibility for keeping the men's locker room organized and that I would undertake any other chores requested by club members, that I would be attired in long white pants that he would provide and a white club T-shirt when I arrived for work no later than 8 a.m. seven days each week, and that my employment would continue until school resumed after Labor Day. My pay for the season would be ninety dollars plus any tips received. The pro advised that it was not customary for club members to tip employees except occasionally at the end of the season.

There were nine grass courts at the club, and they were immaculately maintained by an experienced several-man crew. They had to be mowed very short regularly, and in order to compensate for excessive wear at the net and near the service lines, the positions of the nets were periodically moved a few feet to either side. There were fixed receptacles for the metal fence posts that facilitated the regular moves.

Within a few days of my starting work, the pro's staff was completed (he had no jurisdiction over the women's locker room, which was in the main tennis clubhouse that contained a restaurant and a large ballroom). Jim, his assistant for the season, arrived after completing another year as a college physical education major. Jim dressed as I did, maintained the pro shop itself, gave lessons to individual youngsters or junior groups, and spent most of his noncourt time stringing racquets. It was Jim's second season working at the club, and he educated me with respect to some of the activities, a bit of the etiquette, and particularly the idiosyncrasies of some of the members I would be seeing. On a couple of early mornings when no members had yet arrived, Jim invited me to go on his assigned teaching court next to the pro shop and volley with him. It was my introduction to play on a grass court.

Aside from a few days when I was somewhat incapacitated by a burned sole on one of my feet, acquired when I stepped on a hot coal not adequately buried in the sand after a late-evening beach party with friends, my entire summer went very smoothly. Most of the middle-aged gentlemen who made up the bulk of the male players were very pleasant and required little attention other than fetching additional clean towels. A few of them, after a game, couldn't wait to get to the clubhouse and sent me to the bar to get them drinks, but that did not occur too often since the practice was discouraged. A couple of players kept a private stock in their lockers so that they could entertain their matchmates. The most significant task I was given during the season was that two regular foursomes presented me with phone lists of their groups and occasionally contacted me with the request that I call and remind their group of a scheduled game. Before many weeks I knew all of the regulars by name, and they were all calling me Jack. One of the regulars was a medical doctor, and when I showed up with my scorched foot, he insisted on examining it and treating it.

While there were a lot of vivacious young girls playing at the club during the summer of 1941, there was a dearth of college-age boys. The draft and enlistments had already taken a heavy toll, and the few regulars spent most of their locker-room time solemnly discussing the progress of the war in Europe and their individual military plans. Jim also discussed these subjects with me. He hoped to finish college before entering service. Being only fifteen years old, and with another year of high school to go, I was not much concerned about the draft or enlistment.

The high point of the Tennis Club's season came the two weeks before the U.S. Tennis Championships, then played on grass courts at the Forest Hills Tennis Center in New York City in late summer. Each year before Forest Hills, a men's tournament was played at the plush Meadow Club in Southhampton, and a women's tournament was scheduled at the Maidstone Club. Virtually all of the leading players participated in these warm-up tournaments. The players were hosted in many of the mansions of these resort communities, where they were able to do a lot of socializing. Of course, in 1941 Forest Hills was still an amateur contest. The days of participation by professionals and open championships had not yet arrived. While a few courts were still reserved for members during the big tournament, most of the courts were needed for tournament play, and large crowds (members and friends) observed many of the matches.

The high point of my season also occurred during the tournament. I was impressed seeing all of the top women players up close, but my big moment arrived when I met Louise Brough, a sixteen-year-old who had won a girls' championship and had thereby qualified for Forest Hills. As our tournament was about to open, when I arrived for my job in the morning, she would be on one of the practice courts hitting a bucket of tennis balls. Finally, the pro suggested to me that I go out and shag the balls for the young lady, and I gladly undertook the assignment. She was looking for me again the next morning, and she suggested that, instead of throwing the balls back, I get a racquet and hit them back. Jim let me use a loaner from the pro shop, and for a couple of additional mornings until she had to play her first tournament match we had a good time volleying back and forth. I never saw Louise again after the tournament, but I followed her progress as she became a star and won the Wimbledon title three times in the late 1940s.

When I returned to high school after Labor Day, I presented our tennis coach with a gift from the tournament sent by the Maidstone pro for use during our next season. It consisted of eight cardboard boxes each containing a dozen barely used balls (they only had some grass stains). I was sure they were enough to supply the team for its entire season, even though Wright & Ditson balls were made specifically for play on grass.

Promptly after Labor Day, I again became part of the high school football squad preparing for another season. My season, however, was very short;

immediately after the opening game of the season, I departed with my family to Rochester. Having joined the John Marshall High School class in midterm, I engaged in no sports there. I seriously doubt I could have made the football squad at Marshall anyway, since the Marshall student body was many times the size of East Hampton and the conference of large Rochester high schools played a much higher level of football than we played in Suffolk County.

Despite my doubts about my ability, I decided to try out for the freshman football squad when I entered the University of Rochester in September 1942. Freshman orientation week actually was at the end of August, and the tryouts occurred then. While I was still not seventeen, I had put on a little weight, and I shined in the sprints conducted at the outset of the tryouts. As a result, I was designated to practice for the position of running guard on the single-wing formation adopted by the coach. After I ran down the expected star halfback in the open field during a scrimmage, the coach also decided to have me try out as a linebacker (like a number of others on the squad, he had played for one of Rochester's high school teams). During our short season involving two other college frosh teams, a post–high school military academy, and a similar agricultural school, I ended up playing both offense and defense. As a result, I got physically mauled a couple of times, including such damage to my nose that I ended up in the U of R hospital twice. The second time was after our season was over and was arranged by the athletic department doctor so that I could pass the physical to enlist in the army.

My father actually came and watched the two home frosh games in which I played. I was still living at home and commuting to the campus, which required two lengthy bus rides. My mother obviously disapproved of my engaging in the sport, but she accepted my decision to play. However, she never attended any of my games.

My tennis and football were both suspended from August 4, 1943, until February 26, 1946, the period I was in the army and air corps. The nearest actions related to a sport during that period occurred while I was training to be an aerial armorer-gunner at Lowry Field in Denver, Colorado, and when there was an intermission in my training of Chinese pilots at Douglas Field in Arizona. At Lowry, my company of armorer students spent lots of time in classes learning how to handle bombs and their fuses and learning to assemble and disassemble .50-caliber machine guns, the standard weapon on bombers. A few of us became sufficiently proficient that, toward the end of the course, we were successful in a challenge to assemble a gun while blindfolded. To compensate for the drudgery of classes, each day we marched to the exercise field and engaged in some form of exercise. It often involved running around a long track or attacking an obstacle course. During our final visit to the track, the sergeant in charge asked that all in the class who were proud of their running ability step forward. Four of us did. The sergeant stated that the best time for any student since his dealing with many classes was a specified time. He challenged the four of us to try to beat that time, and announced that he would be at the end of the track with his stopwatch. The four of us sprinted at a signal, but only two of us finished the course; we both crossed the line and vomited profusely. Obviously none of us runners had been brought up in the mountains. We were not aware of the challenge of heavy exercising at an altitude of over five thousand feet.

Our classes of Chinese pilots at Douglas were small. We had only six instructors and an equal number of Link Trainers. The course for each class lasted about ten weeks. I believe it was after the third class that a major interruption occurred in the arrival of the Chinese officers for the next class. Not wanting instructors to be idle during the intermission, our commanding officer offered each of us the option of assuming a temporary job in the headquarters or in the base hospital consistent with our rank as sergeants. All of my cohorts elected to accept temporary jobs in offices in the headquarters. Since I felt I had had enough sedentary life, I asked to be assigned to some job involving physical exercise. I ended up leading a couple of large exercise groups each weekday morning and being the lifeguard at the officers' club pool for a few hours each evening. It was interesting duty. For the exercise classes, I mainly used the routines I learned on football squads plus a bit of improvisation. With

Arizona weather, those classes were torrid. Most of the swimmers I guarded from my lifeguard chair at the pool were wives and children of officers. A few of the officers did occasionally escape the heat for a swim at the pool, but more of the officers swimming were Chinese and from our last couple of classes. They arrived as a group and merely swam laps for about an hour. Since none of them spoke English, they obviously could not be sociable with anybody. I only got to go in the pool a couple of times, and fortunately I was never challenged to rescue a person who was really drowning.

The *Rochester Democrat and Chronicle* gave the U of R football team a lot of publicity in August 1946, when the football coach and his staff opened the practice for the new football season with a number of returning players from the prior season plus about a dozen veterans who had played before leaving for service. I regained both of my freshman positions—left guard on offense and linebacker on defense—and played most of the time during all the games on our schedule, except our game at Saint Lawrence University. After the game the prior Saturday, I had been diagnosed by the team doctor with cracked ribs. Since I was heavily taped and excluded from practice the following week, I was not included on the bus for the away game. As was common with all of the veterans on the squad, my enthusiasm for the team that was so strong before service was greatly reduced. I met Betty at the end of the 1946 season and married her just before practice for the 1947 season was to begin. The coach was somewhat annoyed when he contacted me about returning to the squad. I responded that I would not be returning since I wished to spend my time being a husband and to complete my education as rapidly as feasible. I, of course, never played football again, although I did teach my children and their friends to throw a football when they played in our large side yard on Bishop Street in North Haven.

Unlike football, I never voluntarily gave up tennis as a sport. Betty had enjoyed the game as a young girl in Burgettstown, Pennsylvania, where she grew up, and she also played a bit while she was attending nursing school at Allegheny General Hospital in Pittsburgh. There was a tennis court near the cottage on Lake Sunapee in New Hampshire where Betty and I joined Chick and Ray Rapp, newly married, for their extended honeymoon, and Betty and I played on it every sunny day while we were there, with rackets and balls that Chick's mother, who had rented the cottage for them, found someplace. Neither back at the U of R where we both were busy with classes nor working in Buffalo, New York—where I was sent on my job with Aetna Insurance and our daughter, Joy, was born in 1949—did Betty and I have any opportunities to play tennis. Nor did we play once I started law school; spent another year in the army where our son, Jack, was born in 1951; nor on my return and completion of law school in 1953.

In 1954, when Betty and I settled down to raising our family and purchased our first home in North Haven, Connecticut, we discovered a couple of seldom-used courts in a parklike area in the center of town. Occasionally the family would drive over, and Betty and I would hit some balls while Joy and Jack played on nearby swings and slides. My most memorable recollection of those sojourns occurred one Sunday afternoon when Betty, apparently attempting to serve an ace, threw her right shoulder out of joint and I rushed her to the emergency room at St. Raphael's Hospital. Fortunately, a Yale orthopedist I knew was on the premises, and he adjusted her shoulder without a hospital admission being required.

Not until a number of years after Lora, born in 1963, joined our family did we decide to become members of the New Haven Lawn Club and Betty and I got serious about playing tennis again. With our older children away at college, Betty was able to schedule a number of doubles matches with an expanding cadre of interesting players. Lora took lessons from the pro, Lois Felix; played with an organized group of juniors; and developed into a strong competitor. While I was quite busy either practicing law or heading the electric company, I found it very relaxing to play for an hour or so after work a couple of nights each week and for multiple hours on Saturdays and often on Sunday mornings while Betty was attending church and singing in the choir. I developed several very challenging singles competitions with the young president of a local bank, a doctor from Yale Medical School, and Keith Zimmerman, a West Point graduate who had left the service to become leader of one of New Haven's manufacturing companies. Keith was my primary opponent, and he and I would play many always-competitive sets every weekend. Our wives observed from the club's portico.

I never went beyond the semifinals of the club's annual championship tournament because the membership included a number of younger men who had been members of Yale's often-winning tennis teams. Actually, the high point for the Fassetts in the championships occurred when Lora and I prevailed in the parent-child division by defeating a banker and his son. Another high point of our club participation was when Betty and her partner, Irene Wong, and I and my partner, Andy Wong, played on the team selected by Lois Felix to represent the club in the annual interclub matches. We played with a few Connecticut clubs plus the famous Agawam Club in Massachusetts where, when it was their turn to be hosts, the play was on their grass courts. The courts at the Lawn Club were red clay, and those at the others were either gray clay or asphalt.

After enjoying several summer vacations on Nantucket Island, where our only sports were bicycle riding and fishing (Betty fished for flounder off a breakwater in the bay in the afternoons; I spent many hours most evenings surf casting in the ocean and catching lots of bluefish and an occasional striped bass), and a few vacations on islands in the Caribbean, Betty and I decided in 1979 that we should prepare for my anticipated retirement by finding a desirable place in Florida. For a few years while visiting exotic Caribbean islands, I took up the sport of snorkeling. I was intrigued with examining beautiful reefs, but I gave up the sport because I could not convince Betty to place her face underwater so that she could snorkel. I also quit because I really received a scare while snorkeling alone at a reef about a mile off the beach in Ochos Rios, Jamaica, and I met a huge shark that was obviously foraging for his dinner.

After two long trips visiting sites on both coasts of Florida, Betty and I chose to buy a condominium at Isla Del Sol, an island community located between St. Petersburg and St. Petersburg Beach. One of the major attractions for us was the on-site tennis club with a resident pro and six well-maintained clay courts. Betty and I managed to enjoy both winter and summer vacations, usually two weeks each, at Isla from 1980 until 1985 when I retired and we moved permanently to Florida. Plaques on the wall of my bedroom affirm that I prevailed in the Isla men's singles tournament from 1983 through 1986—evidence that I carefully scheduled a vacation each year to coincide with the event. Another plaque affirms that Betty and I won the mixed doubles title in 1983. It was one of the few times when we entered such a contest, since Betty preferred her female friends as her partners.

Our Isla condo did not remain vacant all the time when Betty and I were not in residence. I loaned the keys to my loyal secretary at UI and her close friend, another secretary at the firm, and they had a wonderful vacation in the area. She promoted the area so highly that one of my engineering vice presidents also borrowed my keys for a visit and came back having signed a contract for a condo in the area. When the coach of the tennis team at Choate where Lora was a student brought a van of girls to Florida for a spring tennis meet on the campus of a nearby college, the entire group of young girls lived in our condo for an extended stay. Since the condo had only two bedrooms and one hide-a-bed, the girls slept in sleeping bags on the floor and even on the outdoor terrace. Quite a few years later, when Lora got married in the chapel at Duke University where she and Parker were both attending graduate school, they extended their honeymoon by a couple of weeks staying in the condo.

Betty supervised the construction of a new home on one of the group of islands in Tampa Bay adjoining Isla and known as Tierra Verde, in preparation for my retirement in 1985. We had our own enclosed swimming pool and adjoining hot tub and we continued to play tennis at Isla. In addition, we both again became quite ardent about two sports we had neglected since our Nantucket vacations. We only had to walk across the street from our house to throw out our fishing lines. The catches were good and sometimes spectacular.

The edible catches were flounder, red snapper, drum, and grouper, but we also pulled in a lot of inedible gulf catfish. One day I landed a four-foot hammerhead shark. I carried it to our house where Betty was entertaining a bridge party. A couple of the ladies screamed! Another day I watched as a pair of manatees swam by my dock, but I had no desire to hook them.

The three-speed bicycles I had purchased for Betty and me for use on Nantucket really began to receive heavy use when we became year-round residents of Tierra. Almost every evening we would ride our bikes together. Often we rode out the dirt road to the undeveloped end of our island where we really disturbed some of the many flocks of big birds that still nested there. Sometimes we'd ride across one or more bridges to tour other of the developed Tierra isles. On a couple of afternoons we felt ambitious and rode all the way to Fort Desoto State Park, which guarded the entry to Tampa Bay from the Gulf of Mexico. That was a trip of over ten miles each way.

As a result of my success in the Isla Club singles tournaments, the pro, who became one of my regular tennis adversaries, convinced me to enter some of the U.S. Tennis Association's seniors' tour tournaments, played at clubs on both coasts of Florida during the winter months. I qualified for the sixty-and-over category shortly after I retired, and I also played in the sixty-five-and-over category for almost five years prior to Betty and I moving to our retirement home in North Carolina. Players came from throughout the country to participate in the seniors' tour events, which were weeklong tournaments. They were hosted by most of the best-known Florida clubs and always involving a fancy dinner as a finale. I commuted daily as long as I was playing in a tournament on the west coast, except for the one in Naples where an old colleague from my days heading NEPOOL and his wife always welcomed me to stay in their condo on a lush golf course. I had to stay at motels when I played tournaments on the east coast, but Betty and my sister, Connie, and her husband accompanied me for a few sojourns. I played respectably in both of my age groups while in Florida. I was consistently given a Florida ranking in the top fifteen, but when I received my sole national ranking in

1989 I was number forty-nine. Despite the number of tournaments in which I participated, I only accepted the trophy once. That occurred in a tournament on the east coast where I was amazed when I arrived to see that I was seeded first in the draw. By some happenstance, everyone seeded above me chose to skip that tournament.

After Betty and I moved to Tierra Verde, we finally chose to sell our Isla condo since we tried being landlords and found it troubling. With no property on Isla, we were no longer technically eligible to use the Isla tennis courts, so we became members of an old-time St. Petersburg country club, the Lakewood Club. In addition to a fine golf course, it had eight well-kept tennis courts and a very good dining facility. Betty found a great group of contemporaries with whom to play whenever she desired, and she soon also became a member of the Lakewood women's interclub team. She had a reputation as a tough net player, and her teammates presented her with a colorful tennis shirt bearing the inscription MEAN BETTY JEAN.

While I continued to play a lot of singles while at Lakewood, including reaching the finals of the men's championship one year where I was soundly trounced by a young man in his mid-twenties, I began to play more doubles. The singles final was quite humorous, because I had a large cheering section during the match of most of Betty's and my contemporaries. My opponent was very pleasant and even a bit apologetic for his dominance. At Lakewood I formed an enduring doubles partnership with a retired surgeon from Indiana, Andy Chau, and we did quite well as a team. Not only did we win a lot of club and interclub matches, but for several years we played in the Florida tryouts for the Senior Olympics. As a result, we were part of the teams chosen to represent the state in 1991 and 1993. With our wives along, Andy and I had a great time at Syracuse University in July 1991, where we were beaten by a team from Tennessee (comprising fellows I knew from the seniors' tour) in the semifinals. A problem arose at the last minute preventing Andy and me from traveling to Louisiana State University for the next Senior Olympics in the summer of 1993.

Betty hated to leave our Tierra Verde home when we concluded that we should move to Point Brittany, a senior condominium development three bridges closer to facilities in St. Petersburg. It had been most pleasant having a swimming pool in our backyard, and Betty had loved the many hours she played in the pool with her four young grandsons when they visited Florida. She hated to leave the three healthy grapefruit trees she had nurtured, despite the only soil being sand. She also had enjoyed the tomatoes she grew hydroponically in receptacles within our pool enclosure. Residency at Point Brittany, however, did not mean abandoning our activities at the Lakewood Club, and our new condo building had its own large swimming pool where residents led water exercise classes each weekday morning. Within a few days of our arrival, Betty was an active participant in those classes.

One reason for our decision to move was that Betty was beginning to experience health problems. At first, she was diagnosed as having chronic inflammatory demylinating polyneuropathy (CIPD). For many weeks I accompanied her during two-hour sessions at Bayfront Hospital, where Dr. Coen and his staff administered IV treatments being tested for the malady. Then, after some troubling heart symptoms, she was diagnosed with a large tumor in the left chamber of her heart. Andy Chau sat with me for four hours outside the operating theater at the hospital while the delicate and unusual operation to remove the myxoma was performed. After a long hospital stay and many weeks of recuperation at our condo, Betty slowly learned by gradual steps to walk again. Our children, who had all been with us throughout the crisis, concurred that Betty and I should move to a full-service retirement home.

My Betty memoir relates in detail Betty's medical history while at Point Brittany and after she and I moved in late 1999 to Croasdaile Village Retirement Home in Durham, North Carolina, to be closer to our daughter, Joy, a longtime resident of nearby Chapel Hill. It also tells of Betty first attending—and then, shortly after, becoming the leader—of exercise classes at Croasdaile. When a well-equipped new exercise room was opened at Croasdaile, our family had it named for Betty in 2001 as an eightieth birthday present. Betty continued to lead and enjoy her exercise classes in the new room six mornings a week until renewed heart problems required that she reluctantly stop in 2006.

I, too, was fortunate at Croasdaile that I did not have to give up my tennis. Early on I was introduced to a former neighbor of a Croasdaile resident who played tennis regularly at the Faculty and Staff Tennis Club (known as "the Farm") in Chapel Hill. That neighbor, Cy Matheson, invited me to join him on a visit to see the club and to meet his tennis friends. As it developed, Cy and I made quite a strong doubles team, and for almost a decade I commuted to the Farm with Cy three or four mornings every week for round-robin matches with a very interesting assemblage of ardent tennis players: Cy had been an administrator at the University of North Carolina before his retirement, Bob Johnson had been a professor in the School of Pharmacy, Siegfried Meuse was still the chairman of the Romance Languages Department, Charlie Harper had retired as head of the School of Public Health, and there were many others with comparable credentials who joined our group intermittently. Since the Farm had a rule limiting the number of times one could be a guest at the club, my new friends had me elected an honorary member based on my teaching years at Yale. In that capacity I not only was able to play regularly but to be a member of the club's senior team, which played matches at a number of area clubs.

During my first few years at Croasdaile, I also entered seniors' tournaments (playing in the seventies-and-older category) in Chapel Hill, Durham, Raleigh, and at Elon College in Elon, North Carolina. That activity culminated in my playing in the state championships held at the Olde Providence Racquet Club in Charlotte in the fall of 2001. That tournament was the beginning of the end of my tennis career since I developed a large hematoma in my thigh during my semifinal match, necessitating that I forfeit even though I was winning. Betty and I hurried back to Croasdaile so that my problem could be treated, and I was actually able to commute to the Farm for quite a few more years until issues about my eyesight and my reflexes (both important for tennis players) led to giving up my car and driving. Thus ended my exceedingly enjoyable tennis career.

I derived some small consolation after the end of my tennis career when, almost simultaneously, a Ping-Pong table was placed in a new activity room opened as part of an expansion of Croasdaile. Since that occurrence, table tennis has been my only sport. I have enjoyed many very competitive games with Joy several times most weeks and also a few games with others.

CHAPTER 9

Camping

Betty Jean Conrad and I decided to get married while enjoying a camp at Lake Sunapee, New Hampshire, in mid-June 1947, after the wedding of our friends, Raymond Rapp and Neva (Chick) Morrill, at Chick's home in nearby Meredith, New Hampshire. Betty had served at the wedding as maid of honor for Chick, her army buddy and classmate. Ray was my fraternity brother and good friend. Chick's mother had rented the camp for the summer. It was on a lovely lake near Meredith, consisting of a rustic cabin with basic cooking facilities, a two-hole outhouse, and a small dock. It was the perfect setting for an extended honeymoon for Chick and Ray until they both returned to the University of Rochester after Labor Day to continue their medical educations.

Betty had lived with Chick at the Morrill home. They had worked as nurses at Concord Hospital for much of the period between the time she and Chick returned from their service in Europe with the 134th Evacuation Hospital. The Evacuation Hospital was part of General Patton's Third Army, which fought the Battles of the Bulge and the Rhineland in Germany, liberated Buchenwald, and met up with the Russian Army coming from the north. By June 1947 Chick and Betty—who had become best friends during their ordeal through France, Belgium, and Germany—had each completed their first year of the nursing education program at the U of R. Ray had begun his course at the U of R medical school. I was still a little over a year's credits short of those required to obtain my U of R undergraduate degree.

Except for a few weeklong trips to a girls' summer camp where she slept on a cot in a big tent and a few nights during my bicycle trip through New England in 1939 with Leslie Mulford when we chose to sleep on the ground or a bench in a park rather than paying for a tourist home, neither Betty nor I had been campers in our youth. Of course, we both experienced a variety of camping during our army careers. For a large part of her time in Europe, Betty slept in a tent with five other nurses. Their tent was continually transported to new locations as their hospital followed right behind the fighting units. At times the army would commandeer a schoolhouse or other structure for them. Their final location in Halle, Germany, was in a building that had been part of a Luftwaffe training center. I slept in a pup tent with a sleeping bag while in basic training, but during most of my air corps service I slept in a large barracks with a lot of companions. When I became the ranking NCO at Mather Field in California at the end of my service, I enjoyed a private single room at the end of a barracks building.

Betty and I were married on August 4, 1947, in the Church of the Ascension in Rochester by the Reverend Cole. Our honeymoon was a short trip by boat through the Thousand Islands and St. Lawrence River to Montreal. We only had two nights in the Canadian city since we both had summer jobs and had been granted only an extended weekend off. We stayed in a nice hotel, ate well, and enjoyed wandering around the old city until our boat returned us to its dock outside Rochester. We obviously did no camping on our honeymoon.

Our first camping trip as a married couple occurred after I graduated in 1948. I was surprised at the graduation ceremony to find that I had been awarded the Caldwell Prize for the best work in the English Department even though I was a political science major. The day following the ceremony, I visited the registrar and found that the prize consisted of a check for one hundred dollars. I had acquired a car, a requisite for the job I had accepted with the Aetna Insurance Company, but I was not scheduled to begin a training course at Aetna's headquarters in Hartford, Connecticut, until after Labor Day. Betty and I wanted to take a delayed extended honeymoon, but we did not wish to spend any of our meager resources. When I got the award from the registrar, we went to a

Sears Roebuck store and eagerly studied the available camping equipment. We ended up buying a cooler box, a camp stove, and a pup tent constructed of heavy material with a floor and ends so that it was completely enclosed when the entry flap was fastened. The salesman told us that our tent was a copy of one made for issue to mountain troops during the war.

Betty and I initiated our camping equipment one weekend on a visit to our friends, Jack and Etta Mae Phelan. Jack and Etta Mae had taken me in from the time I returned to Rochester after being discharged in early 1946 and was employed at Eastman Kodak until the time I returned to the U of R campus for the start of football practice that August. They and another couple and their sons camped at a beautiful lake site in New York's Appalachian State Park for several weeks every summer. We were only able to join the older couples for a couple of nights, but the two ladies had a hilarious time kidding Betty about pampering me, including with the meals she prepared.

On our first major planned journey, Betty and I started by visiting my folks in Stamford, Connecticut, for a couple of days. There we deposited all of our possessions from our vacated apartment in Rochester in a garage. We then set off on our quest to find the starting point of U.S. Route 1, the main East Coast highway before the introduction of the interstate highway system. Being in no hurry, we wandered from the road on many occasions to visit small towns, historic places, and scenic areas, and we were able to pitch our pup tent each night in a state park or campground. We avoided the city of Boston, and by August 4, our first anniversary, we were traversing the coast of Maine. For the occasion we found a small inn on the Bay of Maine and had a delicious lobster dinner. When it became dark that evening and we had not found a campground, we took a side road and a dirt path to what we thought was an open field and pitched our tent in the dark. During the night, an animal or bird collided with our tent, waking and scaring us. I grabbed the bayonet that I had brought along for protection, but we never discovered the source of the intrusion. When we woke the following morning we found that we had chosen a field of blueberry bushes loaded with ripening berries for our campsite! After crossing the Canadian border briefly, we returned to Connecticut by an inland route. Betty took a job at the Stamford Hospital while residing with my folks, while I lived during the week in a boardinghouse in Hartford and attended the Aetna training course.

After our Route 1 journey, Betty and I did not attempt another camping trip for almost six years. When my yearlong clerkship at the Supreme Court was drawing to a close, I decided that we needed a quick break while the court was taking a spring recess. Justice Reed was making a visit to his home in Maysville, Kentucky, and I was caught up on my assignments. By 1954, of course, Betty and I had two active youngsters. Joy was almost five and Jack was three. We still had the Chevrolet sedan I had purchased when I was recalled by the army in 1950, but all of our camping equipment was in storage in the garage in Connecticut. We proceeded one morning from our apartment in Silver Spring, Maryland, to Front Royal, Virginia, where the Skyline Drive began. We proceeded down that scenic route to Shenandoah National Park, where we spent two days hiking and sightseeing. At night the children slept in the car, and Betty and I used blankets on a pine needle mattress. The trip had an educational element since we left the drive to visit Monticello, Ash Lawn, and the campus of the University of Virginia.

By the time Betty and I attempted camping next, we were residents of North Haven, Connecticut, and Joy and Jack were students in its elementary school. One weekend we went with our neighbors and close friends the Harts to Burlingame Park in Rhode Island and admired the beautiful ocean shoreline a short distance away. When school got out that summer in 1956, we were more adventurous. Once again we drove to Front Royal and drove south on the Skyline Drive all the way to the Cherokee National Forest, which contained a nice campground. After a few restful days there, we left the drive and drove past Fontana Dam and reservoir down through Georgia into Florida. In Florida, there being no apparent campsites, we stopped only at Ocala to visit Silver Springs and take the kids for a ride on a glass-bottom boat. We had to stay at motels as we traversed Florida's west coast and crossed the Tamiami Trail to Miami Beach. Since the motels where we had stopped were very reasonable with a dearth of tourists in July, we stopped at a nice motel in Miami

Beach with a swimming pool only a block from the Atlantic Ocean and asked about rates. It was called the Duane. The owner offered to rent us a nice unit with cooking facilities for twenty-five dollars a week. We stayed for an enjoyable two weeks, and I returned home with an empty wallet.

Since Jack had learned to swim underwater and Joy had become a competitive swimmer while we stayed at the Duane, they were both anxious to return the following summer. Completely foregoing camping in 1957 we brought my parents along on our return trip to the Duane and all had a wonderful vacation.

Not until 1961 did the Fassett family attempt a real major camping trip. We had taken long traveling vacations each year, but without camping. In 1958 we again took my folks and visited Betty's folks in Pennsylvania before skirting Chicago and traversing the Black Hills and the Badlands. We stayed in a cabin in Shoshone National Forest, then toured Yellowstone National Park and Grand Teton National Park. Having traveled so far, we all decided that we might as well also visit Salt Lake City and Disneyland in California. We, of course, had to stay at motels every night, but Betty and my mother managed to improvise most of our breakfasts and dinners.

In 1959, with a construction project for an addition to our Bishop Street house under way, we drove north when school let out to see the power project at Niagara Falls and the St. Lawrence Seaway project while we awaited the setting of the concrete that had been poured for the new foundation. In 1960 we drove to New Orleans with stops at a lot of Revolutionary and Civil War battlefields and at Mammoth Cave National Park. We did no camping on either of these trips.

To prepare for a major camping endeavor in 1961, Betty and I purchased a new umbrella-type tent that was large enough to sleep all four of us, if necessary. As it developed, except for a couple of really stormy nights in the Rockies, Joy and Jack were both happy to occupy their own pup tents. We had acquired a second and third ones to add to our 1948 acquisition. We departed the very day school was dismissed for summer, and arrived at a campsite in Catskill State Park in New York early enough to cook our dinner in daylight. The next day we visited Old Fort Niagara and crossed into Canada. We returned to the United States and crossed the Mackinac Bridge to arrive at a spacious state park campground on the upper peninsula of Michigan. Once again, we traversed the Black Hills and Badlands before reaching our destination at Two Medicine campground in Glacier National Park. During our week at the idyllic site, we did a lot of hiking and saw a great variety of animals in the wild. Because it got very chilly as soon as the sun disappeared behind the peaks to our west, we had to prepare our dinner late in the afternoon. We would then all retreat to the large tent to play games or read. One morning when we opened the flap of our tent to start preparing breakfast, there were four inches of snow on the ground despite it being July. Nevertheless, we had an adventurous and enjoyable vacation.

We took our last real camping trip after school recessed in 1962. This time we packed all of our gear and headed east instead of west. Our usual historical lesson was presented early when we stopped to see the Lexington and Concord sites and read about those very important battles. Our first campsite was at Maine's Bradbury State Park. From there we continued to our first major destination, Acadia National Park. At that location on the Maine coast we pitched our tents for several days. Among our exciting activities while exploring the trails and waterfront around Acadia were a climb up the rugged rock face of Cadillac Mountain and a swim by three of us in the frigid water of the Atlantic Ocean. We next proceeded by ferry from Bar Harbor to the uninviting shore of Nova Scotia. We spent seven mostly rainy days circling Nova Scotia and exploring its sights while camping at a variety of remote locations since there were few real campgrounds on the island. There was one campground high above the harbor with a great view of Halifax, but our first night we resorted to camping in a field near a long fishing wharf and another night we camped in a field near the ancient fort at Louisburg. We were astounded when we visited the fishing pier early in the morning and saw huge hauls of codfish being unloaded from many relatively small oceangoing fishing boats. It was foggy and damp throughout our visit to Nova Scotia, so we welcomed our few opportunities to get indoors. We visited the Alexander Graham Bell Museum and Grand Pre National Park. The park celebrated Evangeline and the expulsion of the French Acadians from Nova Scotia after the French and Indian War. Because of the rain and fog, we had seen none of the famous views as we circled the Cabot Trail on Cape Breton Island in the north of Nova Scotia, so we were relieved when we arrived at Fundy National Park in New Brunswick on the Canadian mainland, where we enjoyed some sunshine. Our tents, which had not been dry for a week, were finally able to dry. At Fundy we did a lot of hiking and game playing as well as observing the famous large tidal changes in the Bay of Fundy. Then we scooted back to North Haven.

Our family camping adventures were much modified by the arrival of Lora on April 5, 1963, nine months after our return from Nova Scotia. We introduced Lora to the joy of camping by trying a different kind of trip. When she was still just a tot learning to walk, we rented a small trailer that contained one bed and cooking facilities and departed immediately for the Outer Banks of North Carolina after Joy and Jack's summer vacations began. Another innovation that year was that Joy was accompanied by a girlfriend, and they got the umbrella tent since Betty, Lora, and I could sleep in the trailer. We found an ideal campsite not far from a parking spot for the trailer at Frisco Beach. The swimming, sunning, fishing, and crabbing for blue crabs were excellent, and on a boardwalk from the beach to the parking area where Lora enjoyed demonstrating her walking and running skills. One of the attributes of the Frisco campground was that it provided clean restrooms and a laundry room. The latter enabled Betty to keep up with the need for clean diapers. Pampers had not yet been invented.

Upon leaving the Outer Banks, we visited a campground on the shore of the James River near Williamsburg, Virginia, so that we could visit that historic site. Unfortunately, our first night there, the skies really opened up, and both of the tents became flooded with six inches of water. Everyone had to be wedged into the small trailer. We had one more disaster before we got home when a wheel flew off the rear of the trailer as we drove through Maryland. Despite the disasters, it was a wonderful as well as memorable vacation.

We took one additional short camping trip before we undertook our final major trip. For the Memorial Day long weekend the year following Frisco, we decided to try camping without a trailer. A new bridge to Assateague Island off the Maryland coast had just been opened, and there was a campground on the island. I reclaimed the umbrella tent for Betty, Lora, and myself, and Joy and Jack were relegated to their pup tents. There was one change since Jack had to share the older pup with Joy's boyfriend and future husband, Paul, who had never before been camping. We had a great, sunny weekend, and Paul was converted to camping.

By the time of our final major camping adventure in 1968, Joy was a student at Wellesley College, Jack was attending Taft prep school, and Lora was in preschool in North Haven. The adventure Betty and I planned was quite different from those in the past, since it did not involve use of our car or our camping equipment. Having learned of the possibility, I made a reservation for a campsite for two weeks on the island of St. John in the American Virgin Islands. Such a campsite included a tent big enough for a whole family, and a cookstove and cooking utensils.

To get to our eagerly anticipated destination, we flew to the island of St. Thomas. There we shopped for enough food to last our stay and boarded a small motor craft that transported us and a few returning natives to the island of St. John. An ancient taxi conveyed us and our supplies from the dock where we landed several miles to our campsite, which was in a grove of trees just off the sandy shore of Cinnamon Bay. En route we passed another picturesque bay, Caneel Bay, which contained a plush Rockefeller resort. Our tents were spacious, with cots for each of us, and we were provided with battery-powered lamps. One thing we were not warned about was that the campground was infested with mongooses that prowled mostly at night and would attack any food that was not completely secured. We quickly learned to place any opened food in a secure bag and hang the bag from a branch of a tree. After a couple of nights, we were used to hearing a mongoose bumping our tent as he explored the area.

The beach and swimming at Cinnamon Bay were fabulous. I had brought along three sets of snorkeling equipment, and in addition to lots of bathing in the warm waters of the bay, Joy, Jack, and I would go snorkeling every day in the direction of a small islet some distance from shore. The water near the islet was full of colorful coral and lots of undersea growth, including sea urchins. That spiny creature tempted Jack to touch it and resulted in a painful puncture of his hand. Betty declined to snorkel since she feared placing her face under water, but Joy and Jack became ardent snorkelers. Our biggest snorkeling adventure occurred as the three of us were approaching the islet and came almost snout to snout with a giant barracuda. All three of us hastened toward shallower water.

Toward the end of our St. John adventure, I was able to rent a Jeep for a day so that we could tour old, abandoned sugar plantations on the largely uninhabited island. We departed St. John by being rowed from the dock where we had arrived to a seaplane in the harbor. The seaplane ferried us to the harbor on St. Croix, a much more developed island than St. John. There we had reservations at a motel named the Pink Fancy. We were told that the title reflected the fact that the old building that housed the motel had once been a bordello. The motel had a good swimming pool and cooking facilities. A table near the pool contained a blender where vacationers experimented with making various types of interesting cocktails with local rum and many of the types of local fruit. One night we had a delicious fresh seafood dinner thanks to one of our neighbors, a vacationing air force officer and his wife, who had gone fishing that day.

Our last snorkeling on our final camping trip occurred when we were driven to the National Underwater Park off St. Croix. Joy, Jack, and I were amazed at the massive coral and other underwater features of that attraction, but, although she donned a mask and flippers, I still could not convince Betty to put her face down in the water.

The Virgin Islands escapade was a fabulous culmination to our camping days. Betty and I were pleased to observe that when Joy and Jack grew up, they retained the camping instinct and took many trips of their own, passing on to our grandsons a love of roughing it outside, sleeping in tents under the stars, and enjoying wild and beautiful places.

DECEMBER 1953

CHAPTER 10

My "Presidential" History

"Cool" Calvin Coolidge was president at the time of my birth in January 1926. I was too young to be aware of either him or his successor, Herbert Hoover, in any memorable respect. However, as a youngster I became acutely aware of Hoover's successor, Franklin Delano Roosevelt, for several reasons. In the first place, radios were just coming into common use in homes, and FDR became the first master of the radio address. My parents allowed my sister and me to join them sitting around our radio and eagerly listening to each of FDR's fireside chats. The second reason for my feeling of attachment to FDR was that we shared a birth date. As a result, my January 30 birthday became virtually a national holiday, which ultimately became March-of-Dimes Day to raise funds for fighting poliomyelitis, FDR's affliction, which I had also been diagnosed with at age seven, but luckily recovered from after almost a year of incapacity without lasting effects (I missed a year of school, but having a former schoolteacher mother, the result was being given credit for two grades when I returned). The final thing that FDR and I had in common was being stamp collectors. His hobby was widely publicized, and possibly because of that publicity, I became an ardent stamp collector at an early age and even organized a stamp club of playmates that met regularly for a year or two.

I never met FDR or his wife, Eleanor, although I did once drive my wife and two older children to explore Hyde Park when they were teenagers. I listened to FDR's "day that will live in infamy" address after Pearl Harbor while I was a senior in high school. FDR was serving his third term when I enlisted in the army as soon as I finished my first year of college while still seventeen. Theoretically I was not old enough to vote during any of his four presidential campaigns, but, to my amazement, while I was a private stationed at Cornell University in the fall of 1943 I received an absentee ballot from the town clerk of my small hometown (I suspect such ballots were sent to everyone on the impressive plaque of local servicemen outside the town hall), so I filled it out and sent it back.

My first legitimate presidential vote occurred in Rochester, New York, on election day 1948 after Betty and I were married and both attending the U of R. I distinctly recall the heated discussions regarding the candidates preceding the election in my favorite political science course. I was not bashful about announcing that I intended to vote for Harry Truman since (like many World War II vets) I admired his guts in approving the use of the atom bomb and ordering the integration of the armed services. I did not get to meet Harry during his presidency, but I had the good fortune not only to shake his hand but to converse with him for a few minutes when he entered my office in the chambers of Associate Justice Stanley Reed, for whom I was clerking in 1953, while making visits to not only my boss but also two other old political friends, Justices Sherman Minton and Harold Burton. Harry had come to Washington to attend the funeral the prior day at the National Cathedral of another old political friend, Chief Justice Fred Vinson, who had died on September 8, 1953.

All of the justices and their clerks attended the impressive Vinson funeral, and since my boss was senior among the justices, he occupied the second row aisle seat immediately behind the Vinson family. As Reed's senior clerk, I occupied the aisle seat immediately behind him. All of the rows across the aisle were occupied by dignitaries with the first row containing President Eisenhower and Mamie, Vice President Nixon and Pat, and Harry (Bess did not make the trip). Many times subsequently I couldn't resist bragging about the occasion when I had three presidents within spitting distance.

My amazing year at the Supreme Court also provided the occasion for Betty and me not only to meet but to have a brief conversation with Ike and

Mamie. Much to our surprise, in mid-November 1953 we received an impressive engraved invitation to attend a reception at the White House on December 1. Betty selected a beautiful new dress and elbow-length white gloves, and I rented a formal outfit of tails and dress shirt. As we approached Ike and Mamie in the line (consisting of justices and their wives, congressmen from the Judiciary Committees and their wives, and other court personnel), the military aide charged with introducing us ascertained that Betty had been a combat nurse in France, Belgium, and Germany and that I was also a veteran. He whispered these facts to the president, and as a result we not only got to shake Ike's hand, but to hold up the line for a short time while Ike asked Betty about her experience.

It was a long time after that momentous event before I met another president. I never met Jack Kennedy, Lyndon Johnson, or Richard Nixon. However, during Nixon's second term and before the Watergate scandal I unexpectedly met his unexpected successor. While still practicing law in New Haven in 1973 I had to make a quick trip to Washington for a client. When I boarded my commuter flight from Bridgeport Airport, I was seated on the aisle of the first row when Gerry Ford boarded and took the window seat next to me. He was still in Congress and had been in New Haven for a meeting at Yale. He had a pile of reading materials, but we managed to converse regarding our respective backgrounds and destinations. When, upon my return, I described my flight companion to Betty, I noted primarily his impressive size and that, when he put his legs up, that with his black, well-shined shoes, he wore black socks held up by garters similar to those my father had always worn.

My first presidential command appearance was with Jerry's successor, Jimmy Carter. By 1976 when Jimmy defeated Jerry for a full term, I had become very active in the electric utility industry as president of United Illuminating Company and as an active participant on several regional and national organizations of the investor-owned utility industry. In the latter capacities I was "requested" to attend a meeting with President Carter and his energy advisors to discuss the recurring national energy crises. As directed, I arrived at the west wing of the White House and was escorted to a conference room where Jimmy shook hands with each in our small group, said a few words, and departed, leaving us to talk for a couple of hours. Betty had accompanied me to Washington and had examined much of the contents of a Smithsonian satellite near the White House by the time I returned for her.

In 1979 I began the first of my two one-year terms as chairman of the Greater New Haven Chamber of Commerce. One of the tasks of the chairman each year was participating in the planning for the chamber's annual dinner, which was one of the major events in the community. As I recall, during my first year, one of the members who had a contact arranged for Senator William Proxmire, a hound about government waste, to be the featured speaker. During my second year, one of my business associates and a close friend inquired how I would like to have one of his old Yale friends who had once been our nation's ambassador to the United Nations and more recently been head of the CIA as annual speaker. My newspaperman friend noted that the individual was a former Yale baseball player, son of a former Connecticut senator, and still had a number of relatives in the New Haven area. I readily accepted the offer to take care of arrangements; George H. W. Bush arrived for our cocktail party and sat between Betty and me at the head table for the big event.

During cocktails George learned from Betty that when I began Yale Law School in 1949 we had had the good fortune of being housed in one of the ten apartments Yale had created in an impressive old mansion at 37 Hillhouse Avenue (adjoining the residence of Yale's president) for World War II veterans with children. Since George, Barbara, and their first son (who was born in Yale–New Haven Hospital) also had occupied one of the apartments at 37 Hillhouse prior to his graduation in 1948, George was most interested in our experience there, and his conversation with Betty continued at the table until it was almost time for him to orate. Our table mate, of course, became Ronald Reagan's running mate for the vice presidency in 1980 and ran for and won a term in the White House in 1988. The 37 Hillhouse Bush baby, whom I never saw, of course, also won two terms in the White House in 2000 and 2004.

My varied affiliations (former student, lecturer, legal advisor) at Yale were also the channel for my meeting George H. W. Bush's successor, Bill Clinton, who was elected in 1992 and 1996. One of the required first-year courses for every Yale Law School student was known as Moot Court. Students were assigned adversarial positions on specific legal problems for which they were required within strict time and length limitations to produce written briefs and prepare oral arguments. The oral arguments were held in a realistic courtroom at the school and normally scheduled in the evening since actual judges (usually from New York City or Connecticut) presided over the arguments and generally also volunteered to participate in a critique thereafter. Occasionally over the years, a judge who had agreed to preside would have some kind of last-minute crisis that prevented him from attending. I worked in town and on a few occasion agreed to be an emergency substitute.

In the role of such a substitute judge I was first introduced to one of the Clintons, who was then still Hillary Rodham, a very bright, bespectacled, and very serious advocate, who I observed chose to wear little or no makeup. During the critique session, I learned that Hillary had graduated from Wellesley in 1969, so we discussed the fact that my older daughter was also a student there and due to graduate in 1971. If Bill Clinton was present during the arguments or critique, I was not aware of him (a number of uninvolved students observed both).

The next time I saw Hillary, Bill was very much in attendance. They had been married about five years and Bill was serving as governor of Arkansas (he served for the first time from 1979 to 1981). He returned to Yale to be the speaker at a meeting of alumni associations. I had only a brief contact with Bill during the festivities (cocktails and dinner) in Woolsey Hall, and both Betty's and my reaction was that he talked too long about his plans for enhancing education in Arkansas (he had not yet become the able orator of later years).

I regret to say that my path and that of President Obama never even came close to crossing.

June 18, 2014

CHAPTER 11

The Trip

Joy and Paul picked me and my luggage up at Croasdaile Village at 9:30 in the morning on Monday, June 16, 2014, to proceed to Jack's home in Washington Grove, Maryland, where I would reside during the trip to the Capitol and Arlington. The key reason for the trip was to deliver Betty's ashes to Arlington National Cemetery for the inurnment ceremony scheduled for June 18, but my thoughtful children also had made plans to take me to see a number of sights in the Washington area I had never seen as well as to revisit some other sights.

Our trip from Durham to Washington Grove was rapid and efficient, but rarely scenic and sometimes very congested. We traversed the fast interstate highway route made up of Route 85 to Route 95 to Route 495 to Route 270. The Shady Grove Road exit from Route 270 is only about a mile from Jack's home on Ridge Road in Washington Grove. Jeffrey, who had previously been visiting friends in the Baltimore area, was already at Jack's when we arrived.

My only reactions to the trip through Virginia and around Washington by interstates were: (1) I would like to own the company providing the concrete panels being installed to create high fences all along the interstate highways. I assume they provide insulation to some of the nearby areas from traffic noise, but the thousands of panels all appear to be identical. (2) I was amazed at how few American-made automobiles I saw along the highway. And (3), I am sure glad Betty and I decided against settling in the D.C. area after my year at the

Supreme Court. I would find dealing with the heavy traffic on all of the streets in the area much too frustrating!

I had not visited Jack and Mimi's home since early in the century when Betty and I had attended William's graduation from Montgomery-Blair High School. Jack showed me the many changes they had accomplished to their home and lot. Their new bathrooms and the deep-well air conditioning and heating system are impressive. The latter reminded me of the very innovative system installed for the UI building on 80 Temple Street in New Haven, Connecticut.

While Washington Grove still retains some of its origin as a religious summer retreat for Washingtonians, the greatest change since my last visit was the development on the large lot across Ridge Road from Jack's home of many substantial new residences with a few still under construction. Since the Shady Grove terminus of the Washington Metro system had already been established when I last visited, the area had already begun to citify. Now, however, the whole area is part of the metropolis.

Jack had bought a bottle of Heaven Hill, so I was able to enjoy my nightly bourbon sour prior to enjoying a delicious meal of brisket of beef prepared by Mimi. Since Jeff and I had Caleb's and William's rooms for sleeping, Joy and Paul retreated to a nearby Comfort Inn for the visit. I was quite ready for a short session with my Nook (still reading Atkinson's *History of World War II*) and slumber at nine o'clock.

On Tuesday, Jack demonstrated his prowess in navigating Capitol traffic by finding a parking space on a street adjacent to the World War II Memorial, which I was eager to view for the first time. It is indeed impressive! As we walked around the part dedicated to the War in Europe, I saw the names of the Battle of the Bulge and the Battle of Rhineland for which Betty's unit won battle stars carved in impressive blocks of granite. We found the tall blocks for New York and Pennsylvania among those surrounding the memorial, and photos were snapped at them also.

Jack next drove across the bridge over the Potomac to a parking lot adjoining the entrance to Arlington National Cemetery. Since we were passing an information booth, I stopped briefly to reconfirm my understanding of our arrival procedure on Wednesday. We then proceeded to the Women's Memorial (more completely titled the Women in Military Service for America Memorial). Betty and I had visited the memorial shortly after it opened when we last visited Arlington Cemetery and made our decision about being jointly inurned in the Columbarium. After viewing some of the exhibits, we typed Betty's name into the Memorial Register. It is a computerized, interactive database that records for history the name, service information, photograph, and memorable experiences of registered women. After viewing the monitor, I went to a counter and, for a fee, a large copy of Betty's page from the register was printed for me. We also visited the gift shop (there is always one), and I purchased a book titled *A History of the U.S. Army Nurse Corps*, published by the University of Pennsylvania Press in 1999. I had looked for such a tome when I was writing my *Betty* book, but obviously had not researched thoroughly.

After the memorial, Jack navigated the scenic route along the Potomac to Route 270 and we returned to Washington Grove. We ate dinner in an interesting restaurant in Rockville named Clyde's, which had a New York Adirondack theme in its decor—lots of photos and paintings of Indians and kayaks, paddles and such hanging on the walls. They also served very tasty meals.

Wearing a shirt, tie, and coat for the first time since Betty's chapel service at Croasdaile, I proceeded, with Jack driving again, to the entry of Arlington Cemetery at shortly before one-thirty on Wednesday afternoon. After confirming that we had arrived for a scheduled service, the guards directed us to a special parking lot close to the Administration Building reserved for such occasions. When we entered the building and gave our name, we were directed to a spacious, comfortable private room to await the arrival of all of our group. Right on schedule, Lora was dropped off by her friend to join Joy and Paul at the entry to the special parking lot. In short order, Lydia and Caleb and Lydia's parents, Nancy and Dave Haile, arrived in the assembly room, and Patty, Muggy's daughter, and her husband, Barry, were not far behind.

Mr. Rodriquez, a ceremony coordinator, came in and sat down beside me.

He took the cherry box of ashes out of the red velvet bag and stuck the bag in my carrier. He stated that all the paperwork was in order, but he had two additional documents for me to sign relating to the ashes and the inscription to appear on the niche. He gave me a "Next of Kin Information Guide" and a plasticized permanent visitor's pass to the parking lot and cemetery, which identifies Betty's final resting place as "Columbarium:9:NO5-15-6." When he asked if I had any questions, I merely asked for confirmation that the niche assigned was large enough to accommodate my ashes also. He confirmed that it will hold two boxes like Betty's. I then said that, of course, hers would have to go on top since she always claimed she outranked me because of an earlier date of rank. Mr. Rodriquez and Chaplain Randle, who had joined us, found that hilarious.

From the Administration Building I rode with Mr. Rodriquez, the ashes, and Betty's flag down Eisenhower Drive to York Drive where a shelter with chairs was set up in an open field. We were followed in a slow procession by all of the others from the assembly room, which created an interesting parade of Toyotas. As Mr. Rodriquez and I walked from his Toyota toward the shelter, he introduced me to a lady who had been awaiting us. She was a member of Army Arlington Ladies. She extended personal condolences and handed me a sealed envelope that contained both a handwritten personal note and a card from army Chief of Staff Raymond Odierno and his wife expressing sympathy and extending thanks for Betty's faithful service to the army and the nation.

Chaplain Randle delivered a short but appropriate eulogy and religious service, mentioning particularly the aspects of the campaign in Europe in which Betty's unit had participated. A seven-man battery plus their sergeant standing about thirty yards distant from us in the field then fired their twenty-one-gun salute. Another immaculately garbed group of six soldiers with their leader barking signals then took Betty's flag that I had been carrying and performed the ritual of airing the flag and then tightly refolding it in triangle shape. At that point, a bugler, also some distance away in the field, blew taps, but his notes were somewhat muted by the noise of an airplane from Reagan Airport passing not too high overhead.

With the completion of the ceremony under the shelter, we all proceeded to Court 9 in the Columbarium a short distance away down York Drive. Mr. Rodriquez had explained to me that Court 9 was a new facility that had only recently been initiated and Betty's and my niche turned out to be the top one (niches are stacked six high) on the third row from the entry to Court 9. After Betty's ashes were placed in our niche, an identifying document was attached to the marble cover and a black cover was drawn over to await the engraving of the marble plaque in the form I had approved. A number of niches in Court 9 already contained plaques, but I was not of a mood to determine facts about our future neighbors.

Our entire group then walked down the walkway between the Columbarium courts to a water fountain circulating very blue water and to the wall at the end of the walk. Dave took photos of the group at both locations. Then we all left Arlington for Jack's house where Mimi, Jack, and others provided a sumptuous feast. Jack's neighbors, John and Caroline, whom I had not seen for a long time, visited for a little while.

Thursday was a day of semi-rest for most of us. Jeff had to leave in mid-morning to begin his long two-day drive back to Stillwater, Oklahoma. The FIFA World Cup soccer championships from Brazil were on a Spanish-speaking TV station that Jack receives, so many of us, who were not soccer players, tried to gain a modicum of understanding of the complicated rules of that sometimes violent sport. There were lots of leftovers from the reception, which provided good snacking and eating.

On Friday, Joy and Paul left early to visit their longtime friends, the Simonses, who reside on an estate in the horse country of northern Virginia. The rest of us squeezed into Mimi's car, and Jack drove us into the center of the Capitol where again he found a parking space on the street barely a hundred yards from the Franklin Delano Roosevelt Memorial. Amazingly, as we were about to start our walk through the Memorial, Jack spotted an old friend and his wife emerging with the young couple whose wedding he and Mimi had recently attended. After viewing the FDR Memorial and snapping some photos, Jack found another parking spot on a street two blocks east of the Supreme Court Building, and we all went through security at the northern entry and wandered the halls full of portraits and busts. I found none of Justice Reed, so I queried a docent and she determined that the Reed portrait (financed by former clerks) had been removed for restoration work. The same docent advised me that the very desirable corner chambers once occupied by Justice Reed are now occupied by Justice Scalia. Even with my credentials (former law clerk, member of the Supreme Court bar), the extensive security provisions at the court precluded me from getting behind the brass gates without a prior arrangement.

We all had no trouble, of course, in getting into the gift shop on the lower level across from the cafeteria. The gift shop is operated by the Supreme Court Historical Society, whose headquarters are in one of the old row houses we walked by on our way to the court. When the attendant at the counter in the gift shop learned that I had had a role in the publication of *Black, White, and Brown*, which they feature in the gift shop, he insisted on contacting Clare Cushman, his boss and editor of several of my articles, but it was Friday afternoon and she was not available. Lora and Mimi discovered that there was one last docent's lecture scheduled in the courtroom at 3:30 p.m., so they established positions at the head of the waiting line for us. The waiting line filled fast for, although there were not as many school and other tourist groups at the court as we had encountered at the World War II and FDR Memorials, there were a lot of visitors. The twenty-five-minute talk presented by the docent was well-designed for groups of students or tourists. It covered the three branches of our government, the qualifications of justices, the significance of seniority, the types of cases heard, the role of law clerks, and the history and organization of the court building, and she also sought questions from the audience filling all of the seats in the visitors' section of the courtroom. Of course, the joke about the "highest court in the land" being the basketball court immediately above the courtroom was not omitted.

After the court visit and a photo by Lora of me outside pointing to the windows of the chamber where I not only worked but slept for a couple of weeks in 1954, Jack was able to drive Lora back to the apartment residence of her friend, Jean Flemma, near the baseball stadium in eastern D.C. where she would stay for another night before returning to Seattle.

On Saturday, June 21, I departed with Joy and Paul for Bethlehem, Pennsylvania, where my much younger sister, Mary Lee, and her husband, Sam (short for Floyd), expected us at Kirkland, their Presbyterian retirement home. We drove through Gettysburg, which was full of tourists, and arrived at Kirkland in time to enjoy a tour of the very nice facility. They have an indoor swimming pool, an exercise room similar to that at Croasdaile (theirs also has a director), and a garden where those residents into horticulture can grow their own vegetables. Sam has a plot to which he devotes some time. They have a library and a room where residents can offer products of their hobbies or other items for sale. I saw a number of pieces of pottery and items of tableware with modest price tags. Rather than one big dining area, Kirkland has a number of smaller dining rooms in all of which meals are served by Kirkland employees. They have an assisted living area and a clinic, but no nursing home. The entire community is much smaller than Croasdaile or Connie's and Gunnar's Freedom Square facility. Sam, who is treasurer of their residents' association and on at least four other committees, advised me that Kirkland has about 230 residents as compared with our population of over 600 at Croasdaile. We had a very nice served dinner in a dining room containing about eight tables on Saturday night. Since the only guest room had been taken that night, Joy and Paul stayed at a nearby Hampton Inn, but they were able to enjoy the spacious guest room on Sunday night. I slept soundly both nights in the Wilbers' very attractive two-bedroom apartment. It is very nicely furnished with several built-in cabinets and shelves that Sam had constructed before they moved in.

We were all ready for our beds Sunday night since we spent a vigorous (especially for me) day first playing doubles Ping-Pong in Kirkland's game room, and then, after lunch, touring the many historical sights of Bethlehem. While I had always thought of the city as the home of Bethlehem Steel Company, and it still contains many sad remnants of the old foundries and an impressive unoccupied tall building that was constructed for offices, the city's history is much more interesting than just steel. We first visited the Visitors' Center on the main street, which contains many old homes and an old school established in 1811 by the Moravian community. We then took a dirt trail down to the valley of Monocracy Creek, where a waterwheel and a mill once operated. Eighteenth-century industrial buildings line the creek—in addition to the mill, a slaughterhouse, a tannery, and an ingenious waterworks (the Moravians developed a method of feeding water from the creek through pipes to the town). One of the interesting features of the Moravians was that all of the women lived in a different abode from the men. As we drove around the area, we also saw the more modern campus of Moravian College, where I was assured that the historical segregation does not continue.

Before our trip to downtown Bethlehem, we had lunch from the Bistro at Kirkland. It is open to serve Kirklanders at breakfast, lunch, or dinner with typical breakfasts, sandwiches, or specialty items. Paul and I had the quiche special, and I think the ladies had salads. The Bistro and its art collection impressed me as Kirkland's only advantages over Croasdaile. Apparently there are a lot of artists among the Kirkland residents, and much of the attractive artwork in the halls has been produced by residents or local people. The home has an art committee to oversee the collection and to acquire additions to it.

Sunday night we left Kirkland to enjoy the Wilbers' favorite local restaurant, the Andalusian, which specializes in Greek and Turkish cuisine. It was very good and so abundant that Sam and I needed cartons to bring home a lot of our food. I had an interesting conversation with our waitress, who grew up in Izmir and Ephesus, both places Betty and I visited on our Black Sea cruise. We arrived back at the Wilbers' unit just in time to see the disastrous last few minutes of the United States vs. Portugal World Cup soccer match.

Monday we retraced our route back to Washington Grove. Going through Frederick we viewed Mount St. Mary's College, which I had missed on the way out. Joy advised me that this college is scheduled to be the first opponent of Darby's soccer team at the University of Pennsylvania this fall. My only prior knowledge of Frederick was that it was the location of Hood College, where Azlyn Pflaum, daughter of one of my folks' neighbors in Rochester during World War II, attended. I dated her on furloughs, and we sent letters regularly.

When we arrived back in Washington Grove, our trip to and from one of Jack's favorite restaurants, Alicia's, was far more interesting for me than the tour across Pennsylvania. I appreciated again seeing Quince Orchard Road near where Jack and Mimi originally lived in Gaithersburg, the big NIST (National Institute of Standards and Technology) campus where Jack has worked since getting his doctorate, the meeting hall and tennis courts in the Grove where we engaged in some activities, and several residential streets in the Grove I had not seen since Betty and I once strolled around the community. Alicia's is a Mexican restaurant, and I ordered one of their specialties, Pescado Azteca. When Mimi called the attention of the waitress to the fact that the promised shrimp and scallops on my trout had been omitted, the chef quickly remedied the error and offered a personal apology. We all had dessert when we returned to Ridge Road—a luscious sour cherry pie Mimi had baked from a container of cherries Jack had harvested from their old cherry tree.

After breakfast on Monday, we headed for North Carolina and home, but Joy and Paul opted to take the scenic route rather than the speedy route we took coming to Maryland. At the outset, we traversed an area of affluent-look-ing homes and farms until we crossed the bridge over the Potomac at Point of Rocks into Virginia. The area of large residences, many of which certainly qualify as mansions, continued as we traveled south on State Route 15. It was horse and polo country, and I actually saw a blacksmith shop advertised in one of the villages we passed. In one respect the farms reminded me of those in Ireland because all of the fields were bordered by waist-high dry-rock walls. We passed hundreds of fields in which the hay had been cut and round bales, many enclosed by plastic mesh, were lined up in many fields and near barns. I saw no dairy or cattle farms, so I wondered what animals consumed all that hay. Such large farms as we saw had large fields of corn still only waist high or fields of soybeans that appeared very green and healthy.

Early on we went by the side road leading to Montpelier, President Monroe's home, and we made a rest and coffee stop at a Burger King in one of the towns. There were many Civil War battlefields along our route, but we did not even detour for Manassas or Appomattox Court House. Further south, we saw a lot of logging operations, and we also saw a few sawmills located adjacent to a railroad line. While most of the sawmills were producing planks and beams, one had only railroad cars loaded with sawdust or wood chips at the end of its production line.

We stopped for a rest, gasoline, and a late lunch at Jack's recommended stop, Fishin Pig, in Farmville. It is apparently a hangout for college students from nearby Hampden-Sydney College as well as local farmers and others. Its six large TV sets were showing the current World Cup match, and our waitress served me the largest glass of iced tea I had ever had in my life. Moreover, she came back to refill it after only a few minutes. Their menu board was intriguing, since they have many daily and weekly specials and they offer many craft brewery brands of beer. My fish sandwich with fries was so large I got a container and had it also for dinner when I got back to Croasdaile. I was surprised that we viewed no evidence of tobacco raising until we were near South Boston, nearing a return to North Carolina.

Before Joy and Paul delivered me to Croasdaile about four o'clock, Paul checked the gauge on his Prius and found that the car had traveled about 1,225 miles since they picked me up a week earlier. It was an interesting and enjoyable journey. More importantly, Betty's ashes have been deposited in their final resting place with an appropriate ceremony. I look forward to joining her there.

Fassett clan at Jack and Betty's Wedding, Rochester, NY, August 4, 1947
from left to right: Connie, Irene, Jack, Betty, Howard, Mary Lee

Fassett clan at Jack's 80th birthday bash, Croasdaile Country Club, Durham, NC, December 2005

Memory quilt made for Jack by daughter Joy in 2012 using his old tee-shirts

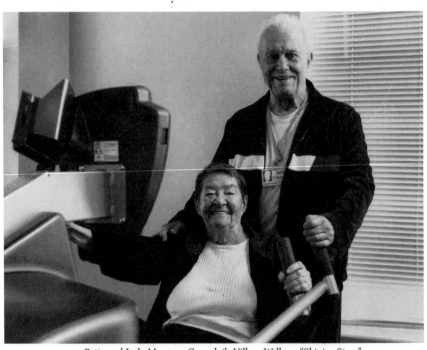

Betty and Jack, May 2011 Croasdaile Village Wellness "Shining Stars"
(This photo was taken in the exercise room at Croasdaile Village where for many
years Betty had given exercise classes to fellow residents. The room was dedicated
in Betty's honor on the occasion of her 80th birthday, December 23rd, 2001.)